KNOCK·KNOCK

Ronald R. Crosthwaite

I0186798

PICFAIR
Publishing

Library of Congress Cataloging in Publication Data

Crosthwaite, Ronald R.
Knock Knock Snapshots of Perfect Strangers
   Includes twenty eight fictional micro short stories based on non-fiction events.
   ISBN 978-0-9898447-1-0 Second Edition

Edited by Rachel Reed
Cover and interior design by
Ronald R. Crosthwaite

ACKNOWLEDGEMENTS

In addition to my editor, Rachel Reed, and countless others who guided me through the process of writing my first book, I extend my thanks and appreciation to the following: Roberta Edgar, Bron Smith, Sheilah Jones, Mark Jason, Bill Smaw, Julian Wise, Andrea Findlay Moran, Brenda Sgambati, Per Volquartz and Ruth Clark who have encouraged me through the years to keep writing. I would also like to thank the Alameda Writers Group for their support during my early days exploring the written word and especially Stephanie Fredrick from the group who believed in my stories saying they should be told.

*Dedicated to
my friend Bill*

CONTENTS

PREFACE

Right out of high school I was in a quandary about what I would be doing in the future. The only answer I could come up with was that I wanted to be an idea man. That led me to study environmental design at The Art Center College of Design and prepared me, upon graduation, to become a problem solver for major architectural and exhibit firms. As an added bonus, I was offered a lifetime teaching credential and taught my craft at Pasadena Community College and Otis Parsons. Solving design problems was my occupation for thirty years, before I became overqualified and was forced to move onto the unknown. Then, through a family member, I was introduced to a line of work I knew nothing about.

As an estimator for a major moving company, I provided price quotes for the impending moves of families and individuals. Fortunately, during my previous career, I'd mastered the fine art of negotiation. The only thing I wasn't prepared for was the stress these folks went through regarding their relocation. I've never thought of myself as a salesman, but as I think back on my former occupation as a designer, I was always selling—ideas, my company, and most important of all, myself.

I became fascinated by the diversity of stories revealed to me through my encounters with potential customers. These personal accounts were too interesting to lie dormant. *There's a story here*, I would think to myself. And I began to take notes.

In my ten years as an estimator, I saw an average of 600 families a year. Not all yielded story material. The twenty-eight stories I've chosen for this collection are the ones I think most beg to be told. Of course, there are still many I have yet to write, but those you will read in this collection hold particular meaning for me.

Allowing me to reflect on my own life's journey, these stories demonstrated the commonality among all of us. They enriched my memories and helped validate the meaning of my own life. We all, no matter what our encounters, take with us bits and pieces of those with whom we come in contact expanding our own personalities and world-views. Life has its way of providing us with guidepost, whether we are aware of them or not.

You'll find that I've included memories of my own life in these stories. Each of these encounters affected me in different ways. I related to the individuals I met and saw the many correlations among us. These experiences also triggered memories of long-forgotten aspects of mid-century American life.

INTRODUCTION

These stories are all based on real events that happened during the course of my work as an estimator for a major moving company.

A telemarketer set most appointments for these free estimates. My job was to create an estimate for prospective clients, and, based on my efficiency, win their account.

The potential customer was advised of my name and the time to expect me. I was to be polite and professional in the hopes of securing their trust. I was also to assure them that my company would do an effective job of handling their belongings. In some cases we had to store their goods in our warehouse and deliver them at a later date.

Our company, as well as our competitors, kept up with the latest technology in order to do the job with maximum proficiency. As estimators, we carried with us a selection of brochures, a calculator, and our hand-held computer that helped us perform a flawless inventory. We also carried a portable printer, which allowed us to leave the customer with a hard copy of the inventory as well as the estimate. Another simple, yet useful, tool was a tape measure, which, in some cases was vital in determining correct measurements for special items or to ensure passage through doorways and on staircases. Occasionally, a camera and/or tape recorder also came in handy.

These appointments usually took between forty-five minutes to an hour, depending on the size of the job. However, there were rare occasions where three hours wasn't enough time. In some cases it was also necessary to visit the destination residence or ask about any unusual circumstances that could impede delivery.

This information, along with an estimate of the quantity of boxes needed for the move, would help determine the cost of the job. This entire process had to be explained in detail to all potential customers. Get the estimate wrong, and it was our responsibility to make it right. We relied on a team effort of drivers, loaders, packers, and the office personnel coordinating the relocation, whether it was two miles or 2,000 miles.

AN OFFICER AND A DISH
1

When I was very young I feared growing old. There I was, only six or seven, and already thinking about my demise. I only knew one of my grandparents, my mothers' father, and I didn't get to know him until I was well along in years. Since my youth, I hadn't had much experience with the older set, so knowing I would be meeting the two elderly people at my next appointment, I felt a little uncomfortable. Little did I know then that getting old was part of growing up and that it carries with it a vast treasure of memories.

MY FIRST IMPRESSION OF THAT FIRST APPOINTMENT of the day was guarded, at best, knowing I was to meet with the elderly couple after having confirmed our appointment on the phone.

Finding my way past the unkempt yard, I stepped onto the creaking floorboards of the front porch. A gray cat curled around my pant leg as I knocked on the screen door. The main door opened slowly, and, through the tattered screen, my first appointment of the day stood there, just out of focus.

"Good morning. Ron Crosthwaite from the moving company. Mrs. Townsend?" I asked.

"Yes, and good morning to you, young man. Please come in."

Mr. and Mrs. Townsend lived in a rather large house in a neighborhood that looked as though it had gone to seed. I was polite and professional, as planned, but I kept my emotional distance as I introduced myself to a woman clearly in her late eighties. The Townsends had lived in this house for fifty-one years and had been married for sixty. Ethel, Mrs. Townsend, did all the talking while Mr. Townsend, Edward, sat in his easy chair, quietly listening. Every once in a while, he nodded his head in agreement with his wife.

"This is a big home for just the two of you. Did you raise a family here?" I asked.

"Oh yes, we have four grown boys, who all have moved on," Ethel said.

"Looks like one of your sons is getting a great babysitter."

"Well, kind of. Most of our fifteen grandchildren have grown, so we're not much needed for babysitting. We just want to be near, in case we need help...it's time, you know." As she was saying these words, she motioned over to her husband, who had nodded off.

"He's got some problems."

"Well I think it's about time your children help out. You must have so many memories here, and I'm sure there's more to come in your new home. Where are your sons now?"

"Edward Jr. is a stockbroker in New York, and, for now, is doing very well for himself and his family. Jeremy is into politics, and lives in D.C. I don't care much for his line of work…he's a Republican, you know."

"He's a senator," shouted Edward from his easy chair.

"Oh yes, a senator, how about that? Edward and I have always been Democrats, as were both of our parents. I don't know what happened to Jeremy, and why he went the other route. But you know, he's seems to be successful…married a fine young lady, and they have four beautiful daughters."

"And your other two?" I asked.

"They're here in California, up north," Ethel explained. "Oh, where you're going, Sacramento?"

"Yes. Cory and Jason are twins and live two doors from each other. Our new home will be just around the corner."

As I began to walk through their home doing my survey, I noticed the usual collection of family photos, and got a blow-by-blow dissertation on each of them. When I entered the master bedroom, the only photos in the room were perched side-by-side on the large antique dresser. The top of it was covered with what looked like a hand-made knitted laced doily that was faded and discolored from the passage of time. A closer look at the framed picture on the left, found me seeing a beautiful young girl with a familiar smile. The girl was Ethel. She was indeed someone I would have taken a second look at, back in the day.

"Quite a dish, huh?" Ethel said, looking down at the photo of herself as a young nurse. She had a peaceful smile that was unmistakably the same as that of the beautiful young girl in the photo.

"And what do you think of my young officer?" Ethel asked, proudly.

As I peered at the dashing young army officer in the photo next to his bride, I instantly came to an understanding that Mr. and Mrs. Townsend had an interesting history. As a result, I immediately gained a new level of respect for this couple that I had seen initially as just two old people on their way out.

"I assume Edward was in WWII?" I asked.

"Oh, you just wait. If he opens up, you won't be able to stop him from talking on and on about his days as a flier."

"A pilot?...I gotta talk to him," I said with excitement.

In the den I found Mr. Townsend sitting at his desk, waiting for me. Photos and memorabilia surrounded him. He proudly pointed out a large photograph of an aircraft carrier that had taken him to war. Captain Townsend had been a pilot at the battle of Midway. He had taken off from the U.S.S. Enterprise and survived the battle, and here he was talking to me about it, which I deemed a great honor. I was full of questions for Edward as he shared his experiences with me. He told me of the air-to-air combat during which he shot down three Japanese Zeros, and was nearly shot down, himself. When he finally touched down on the carrier, he found his F4F Wildcat had sustained numerous holes from the dogfights.

"I've heard how the Wildcats held up much better than the Zeros," I said.

"Yeah, they were tough old birds. One blast from our Browning M2s was usually all it took to take down the Zero."

"Browning M2s?" I questioned.

"Machine guns," Edward quickly answered, as though I should have known.

"I've always wondered how I would have taken part in the war if I had been the right age. It must have been exciting, and yet I can imagine there was a lot of anger towards the Japanese when they attacked Pearl Harbor. I'm sure I would have wanted to be a pilot. What were you thinking when it was time to take off to engage the enemy?"

"You know there wasn't much time to think. You just did your job. Yeah, we were all angry about Pearl, everybody was. We were scared, too. We had good training, but taking off that day to fight the Japs for the first time had everyone on edge. We were so pumped with adrenalin there wasn't much time to be scared. We just wanted revenge."

"I wonder if I would have had the nerve to do what you did. I'm very impressed, sir, and I salute you for your valor."

With that I stood to attention and gave a snappy salute to Captain Townsend.

"Don't sell yourself short, young man. I'm sure you would have stepped up to the plate under such circumstances."

We continued to talk a little more. Then, I had to know the answer to the question I'd had in my head since seeing the old photographs.

"How did you and Ethel meet?" I asked.
"You'd better ask the Mrs. for that story."

Ethel was standing in the doorway wearing that smile.

"I can see why you fell in love with Ethel. She has a wonderful smile," I said to Edward before turning to Ethel. "Well, Mrs. Townsend, how did you meet your young officer?"

"I was a nurse stationed on the big Island of Hawaii, and it was our job to stand by and check out the pilots when the carriers came back into port. You know, to make sure they were all right, and all."

"Is that when you met Mr. Townsend?" I asked.

"I think so. There were so many young sailors and pilots that had been wounded I didn't have much time to see faces. There was so much to do. Out of the corner of my eye I did notice this one young man frantically waving at me, but I was called away to another young man who needed help right away."

"That was *me*!" Edward shouted.

"Are you sure?" Ethel seemed surprised.

"You know I've told you a thousand times...it was me waving at you."

"I guess I forgot. Oh well, it was a long time ago, but we're still at it." She paused, as if lost in thought. "Now, I remember *after* the war when you happened to come into Charlie's Café and I waited on you. That's when you told me it was you who waved," Ethel said.

"That was the first time, but I've told this story many times since then," Edward said, shaking his head. "She can't remember anything."

"And who reminds you to take your pills every day?" Ethel snapped back.

"So this is what has kept you two together all these years," I said with a smile.

Edward looked at Ethel, then over at me and said, "Sometimes it takes a perfect stranger to point out how lucky I am."

"I love you, you old fool," Ethel said.

Just as Mrs. Townsend uttered those words, Edward slumped over in his chair and fell to the floor. Ethel rushed over to him, and, before my eyes, transformed back into the nurse she had been so many years before, attending to her beloved Edward.

I immediately called 911, and within minutes we heard the sirens approaching. Ethel was by her husband's side as the ambulance rushed away, leaving me alone to lock up their home.

Without hesitation, I was out of the door, following the sound of the siren to the hospital. In the emergency room, I found Mrs. Townsend, and sat beside her. She looked at me with tears in her eyes, and said, "You know, I've been waiting for this day to come, although in my heart I never believed it would."

"Is there anything I can do? Make a phone call or something?"
Through her tears, she said, "No. Let's wait. I know Edward isn't ready to leave me just yet."

After about an hour, the E.R. doctor came out of the emergency ward, walking toward us with a smile on his face. "Your husband would like to see you."

"Is he going to be all right"? Ethel asked.

"He suffered a minor heart attack and a nasty bump on the head, so I think it best if we keep him here for few days for observation. Whatever you did before the paramedics got there, I believe you saved his life."

I quickly spoke up. "Mrs. Townsend was a nurse, ah, *is* a nurse," I stammered.

"Well whatever it was, Mrs. Townsend, it was the right thing to do. Your husband is a lucky man to have married a nurse," the doctor said.

Ethel stood up, and with that incredible smile, took my hand and gave it a little squeeze. She said, "Thank you, Ron, for being there."

Then she accompanied the doctor down the hallway to join her beloved Edward.

◆

From that day on I had a deep admiration for older folks, based on the realization we all have a history and a story worth the telling and the hearing. But the elderly have it all over us, since theirs is so made so much richer over time.

When I left the hospital that day, it appeared that Edward had been granted more days of his life to spend with his beautiful nurse, ever reminding him to take his pills. I smiled to myself, knowing the officer and the dish had yet another tomorrow in which to make more memories.

Having met the Townsends, my fear of growing old was replaced with a curiosity to learn what new stories would unfold behind the next front door. Also, what might lie ahead for me—and who might be sharing my last days, reminding me to take my pills.

KIDS
2

My wife and I raised two wonderful children and now my daughter has given us three grandchildren. Grandchildren are great. As they say, you spoil them, play with them, then give them back, and you're home free. I've since divorced and see the grandkids from time to time, just enough for me to enjoy my freedom as a bachelor and yet know the blessings of family. On many of my appointments, kids are part of the equation. But, some situations are just plain awkward.

I WASN'T EVEN AT THE FRONT DOOR, and there I was, surrounded by cowboys and Indians. I had called ahead to change my appointment to a later time because of an earlier cancellation. The four kids were now out of school and I walked right into their ambush.

"Hey mister, who are you? You want to meet my mom? We want a new dad!" they shouted.

"Is your mother at home," I asked.

A little girl of about five or six ran up to me and took my hand, pulling me toward the front door.

"Mommy...we found a man for you," she said.

The mother was embarrassed. "Please forgive my kids. Their father left us a couple months ago, and they seemed to be in a hurry to find a new one. Can we start over?"

"Sure. Hello, I'm Ron from the moving company. And I'm here to give you a free estimate for your move."

The mother introduced herself as Mrs. Forcetti. She explained that she had had a falling out with her husband and while he was gone the kids had decided they were going to find her a new husband and themselves a new daddy. Apparently, they weren't missing their father very much, because he had rarely been home and, when he was, he didn't pay much attention to them.

"Why don't we start in the garage? Most of that stuff belongs to him. The bicycles and the cooler, we'll keep. Oh yes, the freezer, too. All the fish I'm leaving out in the hot sun for him to deal with," said Mrs. Forcetti. "Ha!"

"You think that's a good idea?" I asked.

"You got a better one?"

"Actually no."

When we went back into the house, we found the kids fighting and running back and forth, screaming.

Mrs. Forcetti shouted to her kids. "Out. Get out of the house right now. I have company. Out!"
"Is he your new boyfriend?" the older boy asked.

"Donald, I said, out, and take your brothers with you," she yelled again.

After finishing the inventory I sat down on the couch to write the estimate, and the little girl came and sat down next to me.

"What are you doing?" she asked.

"I'm counting all of your things so we can put them on a truck and take you to your new home," I told her.

"I don't want to go to a new home. I like this one. Are you going to be my new daddy?" she asked.

"No... I'm the moving man," I tried to explain.

"I want a new daddy. Can you be my new daddy?" she asked again.

I was in a pickle with this little girl. She seemed focused on one thing: acquiring a new Daddy!

"Will you have dinner with us tonight? If you stay for dinner, I'll bake you some cookies. Would you like that?" she asked with a pleading smile.

Mrs. Forcetti poked her head out from the kitchen door. "Jeannie, come here. Don't bother the man."

"Mommy, I'm going to bake him some cookies so he will stay with us for dinner," she said.

By now the boys had come in and were standing behind me, watching as I calculated the estimate. They were impressed with the small hand-held computer I used for my work.

18

They barraged me with a collection of comments and questions. "How does that work?" "Why is it doing that?" "That's cool." "Hey mister, are you going to stay for dinner? Mom's a good cook."

I felt trapped, but, more so, I felt sorry for the kids. They were so fixed on my having a connection with their mother.

Coming out of the kitchen, Mrs. Forcetti asked, "So what's the verdict?"

I showed her the paperwork, and she was surprised at the price.

"Hmm, that's not too much. Maybe we'll do this. Can you move us next weekend?" she asked.

"Are you sure you'll be ready by then, Mrs. Forcetti?"

"Call me Donna. Sure we can be ready. Now you're staying for dinner, right?" she said.

"Uh-oh, now the mother," I thought.

"Ah..." I stammered.

"I won't take 'ah' for an answer. Come on, stay. Unless you've got plans...?"

"No, not really, but..."

"No 'ahs' and no 'buts', period. Besides, the kids like you."
The kids were pretty special and the food *was* good. While I waited for the cookies to cool from the oven, I showed the kids some simple magic tricks I did with my grandchildren.

Jeannie brought me some milk to drink with her homemade cookies.

"You can dunk your cookies in the milk. That's the way I like to eat cookies," Jeannie said, smiling.

I was thinking how much she reminded me of my granddaughter, who was just about her age and who displayed the same sweet innocent designed to melt my heart. "How did you know I like to dunk my cookies?"

When it was time for me to leave, Jeannie actually cried. The oldest of the three boys was a gentleman. He shook my hand and said he wanted me to come and visit them in their new home. I promised to try, but I never did. As I drove away, they were all outside waving goodbye. They made me feel so special to have chosen me as their next daddy.

◆

I found out later on that, when the moving van came to load their belongings the following weekend, the kids gave the same daddy treatment to the crew. However, they weren't invited to stay for dinner.

Even though I was now divorced and only saw my two children on weekends, I valued that time as precious moments that would vanish as they grew older.

COFFEE BLACK
3

I learned to drink coffee when I was in high school. It was our job as teenage boys to hang out at Fosselman's, the local ice cream parlor after school to watch the girls coming and going. There, my buddy George introduced me to coffee. At first, I drank it with large quantities of cream and sugar. But each time I got a refill, less and less cream and sugar found their way into my cup, until, eventually, I developed a taste for black coffee.

My love of black coffee came into play during my next appointment at an English Tudor home in the upscale city of San Marino. I knew the area well. I had purchased my first home in South Pasadena, a city just to the west of this posh neighborhood. My former wife and I would go bicycle riding on its beautiful streets, marveling at the large luxurious homes with their well-kept lawns. The streets had been lined with mature elm trees whose crowns merged overhead, creating leafy green tunnels. Showing their age by thrusting their roots up through the sidewalks, the elms created an up-and-down pathway along the rows of elegant homes.

AS I STEPPED UP TO THE DOOR and rang the doorbell, I was ready to meet someone of success and importance. I was not disappointed. When the door opened, there stood a woman of obvious grace and style. She smiled and greeted me with a handshake, but her sad eyes were red and swollen. Clearly she had been crying.

"Hello, Ron from the moving company for your estimate. Mrs. Simpson?" I asked.

"Yes, I'm Laura Simpson. Come in. Can I get you something to drink? Coffee or a diet soda? Oh, I'm sorry, there's no coffee made, but I can put on a pot, if you like."

"No, I'm fine, thank you. Are you all right?" I asked.

With that, she began to sob uncontrollably. As she sat down on the sofa, I moved to her side, and asked if there was anything I could do. When I brought her a glass of water from the kitchen, she just held onto it and stared at the floor.

"I'm sorry. Forgive me. I can't stop crying," she said.

"That's all right. It's none of my business, but if you would like to talk about it...?" I asked.

"This is unfair to you. You don't even know me. I'm sorry, I'm so sorry..." She trailed off into quieter sobs.

"Please, it might help to talk. I'm a good listener," I said, trying to give her an opening.

"He just said 'Get out!'—just like that. He accused me of having a lover, but I've been nothing but faithful to him all these years."

"When did he ask you to leave?" I asked, struggling to catch up.

"Last night. I shouldn't be burdening you with this," she said, holding back the tears.

"Please go on. Did he hit you?" I asked.

"No. After twenty-three years, he just stopped loving me. He said he wanted me out within the week."

"Where is he now?"

"I don't know. He simply said to be gone when he returns. How am I going to get all of my belongings together in a week? I don't even know where I can go."

"Do you have family nearby?" I inquired.

"I have no real family. I was adopted, and my foster parents have both died."

"Friends?"

"I couldn't put friends out with such short notice."

"A good friend would understand. How about I help by organizing your belongings with a nice printed survey of your goods? Then you'll be able to make a quick assessment. Let's get started. What do you say?" I tried to be encouraging.

We got through the inventory in record time, probably because she didn't want to linger over her memories as I did the survey.

"That's his...that's mine...he can have that...I don't want that...oh, I don't know...he can have the damned thing...."

That's how it went from room to room until we found ourselves back in the living room where we had started. The tears had stopped and now Laura, Mrs. Simpson, began to feel anger.

"You've been so nice about this, thank you so much. Are you sure I can't get you anything?" she asked.

"Okay, whatever you're having," I told her.

"I'm going to make a pot of coffee. How do you like yours?" she asked.

"Black," I said.

While Laura was in the kitchen, I heard a key working its way into the front door. I braced myself. In came a tall, dark, distinguished man impeccably dressed in a three-piece gray suit. I stood up and began to introduce myself, but he walked past me as though I weren't there, and headed straight for the kitchen. There was crash of what must have been a pan dropping to the floor. Then shouting, then more crashing noises, as though someone were being pushed against a table and forcing it across the floor, finely a scream from the kitchen I thought about calling the police, but Laura came in from the kitchen, crying, to explain.

"You'd better go. We'll finish tomorrow. I'll call you."

"Are you going to be all right?"

"Yes, he thought you were my lover, but it's okay now. I told him you were here to help me move out, as he requested. He's picking up some clothes, and he'll leave soon."

Just then, we heard a door slam.

"Oh good, he's out the back door." She ran to the front window. "He's driving away. It's all right now. Well, would you like that cup of coffee now? Black, right?"

◆

I moved Mrs. Simpson that next week, and through her tears, she got a handle on her new situation. In a year's time, she called me to move her again. This time, she was getting married again and seemed very happy-- especially with the hefty settlement she had received from her first marriage!

Sometimes when I respond, "Black" to an offer of coffee, I think of that time when I came uncomfortably close to being caught up in a love triangle.

LITTLE BIG ONE
4

I WAITED FOR THE DOOR TO OPEN. When it did, I found myself looking down at the brightest smile I'd seen in a long time. Ms. Peggy Hardy was just a smidge over four feet and had curly red hair. Right away, this made me think of my mother and her twin sister, who were very sensitive about their height of four-eleven. You didn't dare mention the song "Short People" to them or any other reference to their diminutive size.

"Hi. Please come in," she said in her sweet voice.

Her living room was like any of the living rooms I'd seen over the years. I had expected something different, I suppose. As I walked through her home, I found nothing to suggest there was a little person living there.

Everything was noticeably out of reach in the kitchen. I asked her if she had thought of modifying her house to make it easier for her to live in. Her answer surprised me.

"I learned to adjust to the full-sized world twenty-six years ago, when I bought this house. I vowed not to make a single change. Besides, when I have company, I don't want my guests to feel uncomfortable."

She showed me the stepladders neatly tucked away throughout the house that allowed her to live in her full-sized home. I loved hearing her speak. She had a singsong way of talking, and with that incredible smile, she kept lighting the way as we went from room to room while I did my inventory. I tried to keep a certain distance from Peggy so when we spoke she didn't have to look up at me awkwardly. She knew what I was doing, and thanked me for my consideration.

"This is my pride and joy," Peggy said, pointing.

At the end of the hall, was a sacred shrine she'd created -- a small table on which rested a wonderful example of Art Deco sculpture. I had never seen an Erté sculpture, only two-dimensional graphics of the artist's work. It was an incredible experience to see one of his pieces from all sides.

"When you tire of this beautiful lady, I'll take her off of your hands," I said.

Peggy looked at the sculpture, which was just at her eye level, then back up at me, squinted her eyes, and said, "Are you kidding?"

We both smiled, and continued with the inventory.

The coupe de grâce was her office. This little person was very big in the Hollywood circuit. On the wall was a black-and-white photo of Peggy seated on the armrest of a lounge chair next to Frank Sinatra. Everywhere I looked, there she was with that smile, being greeted or hugged by Hollywood royalty. She told me stories of the industry and how so many celebrities had adopted her. Daughter of one of the original Munchkins, Peggy had performed in a few movies, but there hadn't been much call for Little People after the release of *The Wizard of Oz*.

"See that rocking chair over there? That was given to me by Jackie Gleason."

"Was it his chair as a child?" I asked.

"Oh, no! He used it in a stage play, and rather than take it back to wardrobe, he asked to keep it and then gave to me."

Honors and trophies filled the room, testimony to her support and promotion of Little People. She told me that she continues to inspire the hiring of the Little Big Ones within the film industry.

◆

From that day forward I could only view Little People as people who happen to be short.

When I shared my story of meeting Peggy with my mother and aunt, and explained how she dealt with being even shorter than they, I noticed they seemed a little less sensitive about their size.

OFF THE WALL
5

One thing we all used to look forward to when I was young was the circus coming to town. In the 1940s there wasn't much else to compare it with, in terms of pure excitement The chance to see lions and tigers and elephants, eat cotton candy, and hold our breath as the high wire acts flew through the air! The unmistakable circus music getting us all ready for the big show, and the ring announcer who, in his top hat and tails, would always be interrupted by a tiny car that raced out into center ring.

Out of that tiny car piled what seemed like an endless number of clowns, sparking a roar of laughter from the audience of thousands. Each clown had a character all his own. One would spray the unsuspecting crowd with a seltzer bottle; another would constantly fall down or be hit over the head with a giant hammer. Then came the sad clown. The spotlight would fall on him as he would cry watery tears, which he would follow up by pulling out the lining of his pockets that contained nothing but dust. When I see a clown, any clown, the happy memory of childhood comes to mind. This day, I was to meet a clown of a different kind, a clown who had something to hide.

AFTER PRESSING THE BUTTON ON THE OUTSIDE GATE, I waited. After a moment, the gate swung open on its own, announcing my arrival with the musical theme from the Barnum and Bailey Circus. I walked into a beautiful garden planted with local succulents, grasses, and wild flowers of all kinds. Here and there were large and medium-sized rocks surrounded by white desert sand. With its simple, natural landscaping, the garden was peaceful and serene. Ahead of me lay steps leading to the front door. The steps gave under my feet, revealing that they were made of thick pads of blue foam rubber.

Coming through the front door to greet me was a circus clown, a frightening one who resembled the Joker in the *Batman* movies.

"Mrs. Gutierrez?" I asked.

"I'll bet you didn't expect to be greeted by a clown. Yes, it's me, Mrs. Hilly Gutierrez," she said.

"Well, this is a first. No, I didn't. Do you do this for a living?" I asked.

"Do what?" Gutierrez questioned.

As I looked around, I noticed that the house wasn't an ordinary house. It might have come out of a fairy tale. There wasn't a door or window that appeared straight. All were a little cocked to one side. On closer inspection, I saw that it was the frames that were skewed, giving the illusion that the windows and doors were crooked. The house was finished with bright yellow stucco. On either side of the windows were red shutters, and the window frames were trimmed in electric blue. The roof spiraled up into three separate points and was covered with wood shingles of all sizes, as though a child had thrown them up there with no rhyme or reason.

There I was with a live clown standing before me.

"Do what?" she repeated.

I quickly reworded my question. "Do you work as a clown?" I asked.

"I don't work," Mrs. Gutierrez answered. "I'm retired. I'm just a clown at heart, and you could say I live as a clown. After your visit, I'm off to a birthday party."

"How fun for the kids. Do you ever invite them to your incredible home?" I asked.

"Kids? I don't do shows for the children any longer. I do adult birthdays and other special events. Whoever wants a clown to cheer them up, I'm there. Once in a while, I'll entertain visitors at my home, but you haven't been inside yet. Maybe after you see how I live, you might change your mind about visitors."

"I'm now wondering why you're moving. Have you had any luck selling your special house?"

"I'm not selling, just moving my things into storage for about six months while I travel. Come on in, and you'll see what I meant about any visitors."

As I entered the home, I was struck by the intense noise. Birds were housed in two of the bedrooms, which had been converted into large birdcages. Parakeets, finches, songbirds, and two parrots filled both rooms. There were cages within cages, separating various species from each other. The sound of all these birds was deafening. I could see–or rather hear–why visitors would decline to spend any amount of time in Gutierrez's home.

"I'm used to the noise, so it doesn't bother me at all," she said.

"When you move, what are you doing with the birds?"

"I've made arrangements for all of them, except for the parrots. Would you like a couple?"

"No, thank you. So, what would you like moved?"

"Everything else."

As I did the inventory, it was like walking through Toon Town at Disneyland. Fabric of wild colors and patterns covered overstuffed chairs and a sofa. Lavender walls greeted me in the living room and dining room, and silver stars were sprinkled across the dark blue ceilings.

The kitchen was a bright kelly green with mint green cabinets. Each of the pulls on the cabinets was oversized and different in its design. Some were the shape of a white cartoon hand and others were bright red clown noses. Still others were shaped like the various birds chirping away in the other rooms. The stove and the refrigerator were coal black, with shiny chrome handles. The floor was a maze of swirling patterns of colorful confetti. The lights—four naked, 40-watt bulbs—hung on long black cords from a powder-blue ceiling that was painted with puffy white clouds.

"Do you plan to rent out your home for the next six months?"

"No, I don't. I'll have a cousin of mine look in on the property from time to time and keep the garden going. But no,

I don't really want anyone living in my home while I'm gone. By the way, call me Hilly."

"Okay, Hilly. Is there a reason you're putting your belongings into storage and not just letting them stay with the house?"

"This isn't the best neighborhood, and once it's known I'm not living here, there will be looters. I believe everything will be safer in a secure storage place. Your storage is secure, isn't it?"

"The warehouse has cameras and a guard around the clock. It's very secure," I replied.

"Perfect."

The gate swung open, announcing a new arrival.

"I would like you to meet my cousin, Trent," said Hilly.

Trent was a graying, well-groomed man in his mid-fifties. He wore casual clothes, but one could tell from the material that no expense had been spared on his wardrobe. He greeted me with a formal handshake.

"How do you do?" Trent said.

I nodded my head and smiled while shaking his hand. Hilly spoke before I could make my greeting.

"I'm late for my appointment, so Trent, can you finish with Ron the moving guy, and I'll call you later? Ron, it was nice meeting you, and thank you for not freaking out when we met. I'll be in touch if I choose your company."

Hilly left through the back door to her garage and drove away in her late-model yellow VW Beetle.

I turned to Trent and said, "I'll be finished with the inventory in few minutes, and then I'll give you an estimate you can share with Hilly."

"No need to hurry. Did Hilly tell you why she is going to be gone for several months?"

"No. It's none of my business. I assume she's going on tour with her act or something."

"Nothing of the sort. She's going to Sweden for an operation, and the recovery time is quite extensive. That's why her belongings need to be kept in a climate-controlled environment, such as a warehouse. I'm actually her guardian and executor, and will take responsibility for her belongings while they're in storage. What I mean to say is that I will be the one you will be doing business with if your company wins the bid."

"I see. It is a little odd that she only does parties for adults as a clown. Can you shed some light on that?"

"Did you get a good look at her face through the make up?"

"Not really. Should I have noticed anything?"

"Hilly was severely burned years ago, and it took many more years for her to find a way to cope with her disfigurement. If you were to look very closely at her face, you could tell it's not all make-up. She has worked around her deformity with the cosmetics, but since children have been frightened by her appearance, she only lends her talents to adult parties. But at one time, she was very much in demand for children's parties."

"Is that why she dresses as a clown and lives in this fantasy house?"

"Have you noticed there are no mirrors in the house? She can't bear to look at herself."

"How does she put on the make-up without a mirror?"

"From memory. She uses a photo of herself in full make-up, and does it all by feel. She's got quite a good act, you know. She entertains the rich and famous all over the city."

"Why the birds, and so many?"

"They kept her so busy, she didn't have time to feel sorry for herself. But, the deformity finally got to her, and she raised enough money, with the family's help, to have her entire face reconstructed. It's a new procedure, and has only been tried abroad."

"Tried? Have there been any successes?"

"Hopefully she'll be the first. She couldn't wait any longer. It's been twelve years since that day..." he trailed off.

"How did it happen?"

"She was robbed, and the bastards knocked her out and torched the house. She was rescued by a fireman, but she ran back into the flaming house to try to save her infant son. Sadly, it was too late. She suffered third-degree burns over ninety percent of her body, and she was not expected to live. Plastic surgery and over 100 visits to the hospital brought her back from the brink, but she lives with disfigurement and shame. It took a long time for her to find a way to cope with her situation, and now you're in her fantasy. Hiding behind the mask of a clown has helped her get through each day. This house and how it's configured and how she lives her life with the birds and all has been her reality for the past seven years."

◆

My company won that bid, and when it came time to move Hilly Gutierrez back into her home, I was there. I was curious to see how the operation went, just because she was such a special lady. The results were stunning. She was beautiful. Later, speaking with her cousin Trent, I learned that it was only her face that was changed. The rest of her body still held the scars from the past, and it would take many more years and much more money for further treatment. Ultimately, Hilly chose to not opt for more operations, and she returned to being a clown. But, now she felt comfortable making herself up as a happy clown for the children she had missed so deeply.

In the short time I knew Mrs. Gutierrez, I was moved by her love of life. How determinedly she dealt with her disfigurement, never giving up her passion for clowning.

I now know that I will think twice when faced with obstacles along my life's journey, realizing all is rarely lost. Hilly inspired me to never give up hope and to make the best of what is handed me, whether as the cause of my own misfortune, or as the hand I was dealt.

COLOR BLIND

6

My first real girl friend, Diane, was one of the most popular girls at the skating rink I haunted. I was twenty-one and she was seventeen, and still in high school. To my surprise, she actually chose me over all the other guys vying for her attention. After three months of going steady with my dream girl, I presented her with a friendship ring. That's when my world started to crumble.

My mother and I had been invited to a family gathering for Mother's Day at Diane's uncle's home. They were all very fair-skinned and had blond hair, while my mother and I had black hair and dark skin. So as a result of my giving Diane the ring, her father thought the next step was marriage, and he just couldn't have that. Diane's father said that his family started to shun him because of my mother and me. He forbade me from ever seeing his daughter again. My dream was over. I had never experienced discrimination before. It was new, and I didn't understand it. It took me two years before I could wake up without a tear-soaked pillow. As time passed, I learned that some move well beyond discrimination and accept people as they are.

THERE ARE GOOD PEOPLE AND THERE ARE SPECIAL PEOPLE in this world. I met a special person on this particular day on the job. Mrs. Kelly Logan invited me into her home without looking at me. I thought it strange when she glanced away while talking to me, but then I realized Mrs. Logan was blind. She had lost her sight as a young child. To that day, she didn't remember what her mother or father looked like. She did, however, remember their love, and she showed her affection daily to both her elderly parents, as she gave them the constant round-the-clock care they needed. Mrs. Logan had two children to look after, as well.

Her husband had left her two years before, after eight years of marriage. He just couldn't cope with Kelly's disability. Every other weekend he came to take the children for a couple of days, giving Kelly some relief. They had remained good friends, but he still couldn't deal with her being blind. He'd since married again, to a sighted woman.

Moving was the only option for Kelly, because she could no longer afford the rent. New apartments were being built in her neighborhood, and the rents started going up far beyond her reach with her limited income. Knowing where she was moving, I asked her if she knew that her new address was in South Central, an all-black area.

She said, "Oh yes I know. I'm sure we'll be all right."

I kept in touch with Mrs. Logan to find out how the move went and to know that she was making the adjustments okay in her new surroundings. Her neighbors on either side of her saw Kelly as their token white neighbor. They had never lived near anyone who wasn't black. Kelly knew her situation, but she never mentioned a word to me as we spoke.

"I have two new wonderful friends who help me look after my children, giving me more time to attend to my parents," Kelly said.

She saw only the goodness in her new friends, and didn't even think of their skin color. I wished her well and said my goodbyes.

Ten months had gone by when I got a call from Mrs. Logan, saying she needed to move again.

I said, "Sure, what happened?"

"Our little family has grown, and we need a bigger house," she said.

"What do you mean your family has grown?"

"Lilly, my new neighbor friend, was killed in an auto accident, and I've decided to adopt her three children, so you see we need a bigger house and a nice big backyard. We've found one over on 167th street, and I'm going to need some help moving two households. Can you move us in about a month?"

"I'm so sorry about you losing your new friend. Yes, of course we can move you in a month or whenever you say. Are your parents doing okay?" I asked.

"Yes, Dad had another stroke but he's hanging in there. Thank you for asking. Oh, and we've inherited a dog, as well," she said.

"Are you going to manage with so many new responsibilities?"

"We'll see."

♦

If only Diane's father hadn't been so blind. If only he could have seen through Kelly Logan's eyes and truly believed the lyrics of his favorite song:

"It's still the same old story; a fight for love and glory; a case of do or die, the world will always welcome lovers, As Time Goes By..."

SAVING HANDS
7

I found myself in unfamiliar territory, Watts. The streets were narrow and every small house on the block had metal bars on the windows and doors. The locals stared at me as I slowly drove down the street, making my way to my appointment. Many of the cars parked along the stretch of small homes were in poor repair, either dented or in need of a paint job. Luckily someone was pulling out from a parking space, so I quickly scooted in. As a white man emerging from a shiny clean car, that I was conspicuous was an understatement.

UPON FINDING THE ADDRESS, I PUSHED OPEN THE BROKEN GATE and walked up the narrow path leading to the house. I knocked and waited. The sound of scrambling came from inside the house, and then, slowly, the door opened. A young girl of about ten or eleven peeked from behind the door and looked up at me.

"Is your mom at home?" I asked.

She pulled open the door and backed up, lowering her head to shout, "Mom, there's a man here wants to see you!"

I was led into the dining room where a woman sat, very pregnant, greeting me with a beaming smile.

"Hello, my name is Mrs. Jamie Smith, and you must be Ron from the moving company."

She was very polite and cordial, bowing her head as she spoke. I knew right then I was in the presence of a lady.

"Hello, Mrs. Smith."

A lady in Watts, I thought. Her three children came and went, I think to check me out.

"Children, Mommy's got company. You go on and play in your rooms now," Mrs. Smith said.

To my surprise, all three children were very obedient.

"Yes, Mommy," they said.

"When are you expecting your next child?" I asked.

"Few more months."

"I have to say, your children are very well behaved."

"Why thank you. That means a lot to me."

"So, you're moving to Texas."

"Oh, yes. We made a killing on this old house, and we've got to get out of California, especially this neighborhood. There are so many drugs and guns shooting off in the night. I fear for my children."

"Has your husband found work in Dallas?"

"Yes. His uncle has a cabinet business there. He's so happy to be working with his hands again."

"Oh?"

"Seven years ago, my husband was badly burned when he saved a child from a burning house. He's been on disability ever since. Finally, his hands are healed well enough to return to the woodworking he loves."

"How wonderful for him. He actually saved a child. My goodness, he's a hero!"

"Don't tell him that. He just couldn't imagine not running into that house after hearing that child's cry."

"I'd like to meet your husband. Is he coming home soon?"

"You're going to have to wait a while. He's in Texas for another week arranging for our new home. Are you hungry?"

"Ma'am?"

"Have you ever had soul food?"

◆

Without expecting it, I found myself enjoying the company of a real lady. I was in Watts, but I wasn't. It felt as though I were in another country. Mrs. Smith spoke with an elegance I had only experienced in the movies. Her children also had the gift of grace, as they would enter into the conversation from time to time, but only when asked.

This marked the first of several encounters I was to have with black families living in South Central Los Angeles. Each, in turn, taught me a new awareness of tolerance and understanding of a sub-culture about which I knew little.

GIVING BACK
8

It was winter, and the appointments were few and far between. Besides no money coming in, my car needed new tires. There was an unusual downpour of rain on this particular day, and I couldn't think of a worse time to be out on the road. As my luck would have it, the office called and asked if I could do an appointment within the hour. What was I going to say, no?

When I got out there, sure enough, I saw typical Southern Californian drivers continuing to drive at their normal fast speed, causing one collision after another. As I headed down the freeway, a large SUV did a 360 right in front of me. The only reason I missed hitting him was because he spun out of the traffic lanes and onto the shoulder. I knew I had to get to where I was going, and fast—but not *too* fast.

Finding my way to the address in a section of Pasadena that was predominately black, it occurred to me my colleagues would have treated this as an uncomfortable, even undesirable, assignment. But, having had a childhood friend who was black, it wasn't an issue for me. He was our quarterback. My old buddy, Bill, and I would run nearly to the end of the road chasing Junior's passes. He was head and shoulders above us in terms of ability, and not just because he was a few years

48

older. It would be an understatement to say that I looked up to him. We both did.

Junior and his family lived in a little wooden shack across a dirt road from where Bill and I lived with in government housing projects. But you couldn't judge his family by where they lived. Because of that dirt road his father would be out there polishing his prized possession—a 1948 two-toned green Pontiac with foxtails hanging off the back bumper and skirts on the back wheels. The car had a sun visor and two extra chrome side mirrors that caught the sun when the light was just right. You could tell he loved that car. Entering their house, the first thing I'd be struck by was the rich aromas of flavorful food that permeated the house. My home smelled like cereal.

I was aware that Northwest Pasadena was a black neighborhood, although not to be compared with Watts. Not even close. The houses on this block were all kept up, with lawns manicured and curbside addresses freshly painted. Even in the rain the neighborhood looked homey and inviting.

IT WAS AROUND LUNCHTIME WHEN I ARRIVED. Robert Walker greeted me at the front door with a firm handshake and a smile. A tall black man in his sixties, graying at the temples he sported a Dodger baseball cap, a thin mustache, and the whitest teeth I'd ever seen. His home gave the appearance of a woman's touch. There were brightly colored walls and flowered patterns on the furniture along with collections of porcelain statuary everywhere. It was a little overwhelming. As I made the rounds, doing the usual inventory, Mr. Walker asked if I were hungry.

"I'm just about to sit down with my brother-in-law for some lunch. You're welcome to join us, if you like," he said.

"I just had a late breakfast. I'd better not," I said.

"Are you sure I can't tempt you?"

"Well, since you're sitting down anyway, I'll be happy to have a little something…whatever's cooking. It sure smells good. What's on the menu?"

"Mother's cooking," Robert answered with a smile.

We made our way back to the kitchen where I was introduced to Tyrone, who didn't look too happy to see me.

"This is Tyrone, my brother-in-law," Mr. Walker said.

"Hello," I said.

"Hey," Tyrone mumbled, barely audible.

Tyrone was hunched over his lunch like a starving person protecting his food. He had tattoos on both of his shoulders and arms and a Du rag crowning his head.

"You don't have to eat with us if you don't like our food," Tyrone said.

"Hey man, cool it. Ron's our guest," Mr. Walker said. Then he turned to me. "You smell that? That's soul food. You ever had soul food?"

"Yes, as a matter of fact, when I worked in the area, I used to go to Aunt Ady's Soul Kitchen for lunch," I said.

"Hey man, what are doing eating in our neighborhood anyway?" Tyrone said with a sneer.

"Tyrone, I said cool it!" Mr. Walker interrupted.

Tyrone stood up, staring down at me with a threatening look, and as he walked past me, he purposely bumped my chair.

"Don't mind him. I'm not going make excuses for him. He'll be gone soon," Mr. Walker said.

Just then Tyrone yelled at me from the living room. "Hey man, is that your green Honda out front?"

"Don't answer that," Mr. Walker said quietly. Then he called out, "Ron told me his partner dropped him off...he'll be here to pick him up in a half an hour."

We heard the door slam and Tyrone was gone, for which I was grateful.

"Why did he want to know if that was my car?" I asked.

"I don't know. He might have done something to it. I'm pretty sure he won't, though. Please don't worry."

I got up and looked out of the window to make sure...no sign of Tyrone.

"What's his problem?" I asked.

"He doesn't like white people...He had a bad experience in the joint...what can I say?"

I nodded, and gave a small smile.

"Getting back to Aunt Ady's, you know she passed away only a month ago. Her son is trying to keep up the business, but it won't be the same," he explained.

"I'm sorry to hear that. She was such a sweet woman. I remember the first thing Aunt Ady said to me when I wandered into her establishment: 'What's a nice white boy like you doing in a soul food restaurant?' But she greeted me with that warm smile of hers."

"Yes, she was something else. She welcomed everybody, didn't matter what color you were."

"I'd said to her: 'My nose led me to your place. I couldn't resist the wonderful smells.' And it was true—they reminded me of my friend Junior's house, how it always smelled so delicious. Walking into Aunt Ady's Kitchen called back those memories for me. Anyway, she told me, 'When you walk into a black family's home, you get all these good smells coming from the kitchen. When you walk into white folks' homes, it smells like lettuce.' She'd laugh with a laugh that seemed to come up from the bottom of her stomach. Then she would clap her hands and say, 'Okay, what's your pleasure?' I kept going back just to hear her happy greeting and to enjoy the delicious food. She'll be missed."

Then she would clap her hands and say, 'Okay, what's your pleasure?' I kept going back just to hear her happy greeting and to enjoy the delicious food. She'll be missed."

"Sure will."

Even though I had just finished breakfast, the lunch was so tasty I couldn't stop eating. It was like a Thanksgiving dinner where the food is so good you don't care how full you are or how uncomfortable you're going to feel.

After the scrumptious lunch, I said, "I guess I'd better finish with my inventory," and I went through the rest of the house.

Then Mr. Walker said, "Now it's time to see the good stuff, in the garage—my stuff."

As we set out for front door, I accidentally knocked over a small porcelain vase. We both watched as it tumbled to the hardwood floor, shattering into several pieces. Mr. Walker and I looked at each other, our eyes widening.

"Oh man, I'm so sorry Mr. Walker. I'll pay for it. I can send you a check. How much do you think its worth?"

"I don't think you want to know. I got it for my wife for our twentieth wedding anniversary. She never liked it. This is the perfect excuse. Don't worry. I'll handle it. You don't have to pay for it. Forget it."

"Really...?"

"Yeah. I'll say I did it, and she'll forgive me. I don't know if she would forgive you. You haven't met her. She can be tough. But hey, she'll never know. By the way, call me Robert. Ron, right?"

Somewhat relieved, I nodded, and followed Robert out to the garage.

"Now here's my domain," Robert said with pride as we approached the garage.

The garage door was up, revealing a heavy black drape across the opening. Robert pulled it back and invited me in. The ceiling, the walls, and the floor were covered with dark gray carpet. Along one wall were floor-to-ceiling shelves crammed with hundreds of CDs. On another wall, LPs filled the shelves. Two stacks of 45 rpm records were held in place with a couple of wooden poles resembling broomsticks that

53

reached almost four feet high. Two computers and some other electronic equipment were arranged neatly on a long table at the back of the room. A small stool with a well-worn vinyl seat and a comfortable looking leather armchair were the only two pieces of furniture in the room. Large acoustic speakers hung from the ceiling in all four corners. Photos of music icons of the '30s and '40s were displayed wherever wall space allowed.

"Well, what do you think of my place?" Robert asked.

"Very nice. Looks like you have an incredible collection of music here!"

As I started looking at the labels I noticed familiar names: Miles Davis, John Coltrane, Sonny Rollins, and on and on…

"Jazz and blues, and some oldies from my days. Man, this is fantastic," I said.

Robert sounded surprised. "You like jazz and blues?"

"Yes, very much. And you've got some great ol' R&B I haven't heard in a long time."

"Then, you're gonna love this."

Robert put a CD into the player and pushed the "play" button. We both started singing along, tapping our feet.

My baby don't stand no cheatin', my babe, Oh yeah she don't stand no cheatin', my babe, Oh yeah, she don't stand no cheatin', She don't stand none of that midnight creepin', my babe….

Robert smiled. "You know the words to "My Babe" …very cool."

"Yes, but I don't recognize the artist."

"Oh, that's me," Robert said with a broad smile, his chest puffing out in pride.

"You're good. What goes on here? What's with the recording equipment?" I asked.

It turned out that Robert recorded and produced pop blues, but the records didn't sell in the States. His market was in Europe and Japan. He recorded right there in his garage, which he had turned into a sound studio.

"Why doesn't your music sell in the States?"

"They're all into hip-hop here, but in Europe and Japan, they still appreciate the good ol' music."

"Maybe I'm in the wrong country, because I love the good ol' music, too. By the way, you've got a very impressive collection of LPs. Have you got them onto CDs yet?" I asked.

"I've transferred every one of them. See those three cardboard boxes over there? They're full of tapes. I also transferred them."

"Since you've transferred all of these LPs, any chance you're going to get rid of them now?" I was trying to hint that I could take some of them off his hands.

"I can't give up my vinyl, but hey, would you like the tapes? I don't have any use for them now, so if you want them, they're yours."
"You mean it?" I asked, astonished.

"Yeah, you like the music, right? Besides, I would rather they find a home with someone who appreciates good sounds. Otherwise, I don't know what I'll do with them."

Robert Walker was not only generous with his prized collection, but he was also a leader in his community and wore many hats besides his Dodger cap. For one thing, he was president of the Pasadena Little League and had been involved in the Pasadena Youth program for many years. I only found that out after asking him about the baseball bats and gloves I had noticed in the back seat of his car as I walked up the driveway to his front door. But that wasn't the biggest surprise I was to learn about Mr. Walker. His day job just didn't fit this singer of songs, this leader of youth activities. He was head coroner for the City of Los Angeles as well as the main consultant for the TV series, *CSI Miami*.

Now he was stepping down from these diversified lives he had led for thirty-five years, and was retiring. He and his wife were moving to New Orleans, where she had grown up.

"Do you have family in Louisiana, as well?" I asked.

"No, I'm from right here in Pasadena. My family has been here from the beginning."

"What do you mean, 'the beginning'?"

"I mean, the beginning. I mean, back to slavery. My ancestors were taken out of slavery to work on the railroad. They came up the line slaving away until my father joined the *Brotherhood of Sleeping Car Porters* (BSCP). He was a porter for thirty-eight years till he retired in '67."

"I didn't know there as such an organization. What was that all about?"

"It was the first black union formed by the early railroad workers way back in the '20s."

"Fascinating! I wonder if I ever ran across your father in the years I traveled the train from San Diego to LA."

"When was that?" Robert asked.

"From around 1947 to '51. I was sent to stay with my aunt on her ranch in Montebello for the summers. They would pin a note on me and send me off on that big black steam-belching locomotive. I'll bet your father would remember a white kid sitting alone with a note pinned to his jacket."

"I'll bet he would. I would ask him, but he passed sixteen years ago. That was his route, though, for many years."

"Sorry man. Yeah, my dad's gone, too."

We talked about music and the railroad for the longest time, until Robert heard a car pull into the driveway and stopped our conversation cold.

"The little woman is here. I want you to meet her," he said.

"What about the vase?" I asked in a panic.
"Oh, crap. Wait here, and I'll call you for the all-clear. I won't be a minute."

While Robert was doing a quick clean-up and clearing the path for my introduction, I checked out the song titles of the tapes in the three boxes, noticing they were almost identical to the LPs I had been vying for.

"Hey, Ron! Come in," Robert yelled out from the back door. "Everything's cool," he said in a whisper. "Come on and meet the wife."

When I entered, Mrs. Walker was in the living room inspecting the floor, finding more pieces of the fallen vase. Robert introduced me.

She looked up at me and said, "My husband is so clumsy sometimes…nice to meet you, Ron. I hear you and Robert have been getting along, talking about music and trains. That's all he talks about. But I love the man, so what can I do after forty-two years? Can't trade him in. No one would have him."

Then she chuckled with a big smile on her face, raised her eyebrows, slapped her thigh, and pulled Robert to her side, giving him a loving hug.

Mrs. Walker was a delight. Her voice rang with enthusiasm and confidence, with just a hint of playfulness. She invited me to sit down, and asked me to feel right at home.

"Thank you, Mrs. Walker," I said.

"No Mrs. Walker now, you call me "Dixie." Would you like something to drink? I'll bet Robert didn't even offer you anything." She looked over to her husband with a scowl.

"No, he invited me to join him and your brother for lunch, and sample some of your fine cooking. It was delicious, I might add. Water would be great for now, thanks," I replied.

I went on to tell Dixie of how I was introduced to soul food at Aunt Ady's Kitchen.

"Oh that's wonderful. She was the best. I miss that lady. You know what you were served this afternoon was one of her recipes...."

"No wonder it was so delicious!"

"So...water? Are you sure I can't get you something stronger? I'll just get you a cold beer," she decided.

Robert looked over at me, knowing I couldn't refuse. It was clear who wore the pants in the family. As she returned with a cold one she said, "Ron, you like parties?"

"Sure," I said with hesitation.

"Well then, you're coming to my going-away party this Friday. Okay?" After thirty-three years, Mrs. Dixie Walker was retiring as the scoreboard keeper at the Pasadena Rose Bowl.

I accepted Dixie's invitation and presented the Walkers with their estimate. Then, we said our goodbyes. Robert helped me carry the three boxes of tapes out to my green Honda. As I opened the car door, a tweaked out '61 copper-colored Chevy drove by, carrying four young black men, one of whom was Tyrone. As they passed, he kept staring at me. I chose to take a detour home, eventually feeling comfortable that no one was following me. The next day Robert called to let me know he and Dixie had chosen my company to move them to New Orleans.

I was about to hang up when Robert said, "Ron, just a minute. Dixie wants to say 'hello.'"

"Hey Ron, you haven't forgot my party, have you?" Dixie asked.

"Oh no, I'm looking forward to it. And thank you for your business."

"Okay. We'll see you Friday, and don't worry. My brother, Tyrone, is not invited, and he won't be there, I promise."

"I'll be there for sure," I told her.

That next Friday, I joined the well-wishers at the Rose Bowl for Dixie's send-off. The going-away party was to be held in the VIP lounge, where the public was never invited. The partygoers waited outside to greet her as she arrived. On schedule, a long black limousine pulled up and Dixie stepped out in a fancy hat and bright red dress, sparking a welcoming roar from the crowd. The Pasadena Youth Drum and Bugle Corps were there to perform in her honor. To precise drumbeats, they marched around in their blue and white uniforms, their shiny brass horns playing as they danced to the rhythm of their music. Everyone was caught up in the performance, swaying and clapping to the beat. Finally, the band led Dixie to the entrance of the building as we all filed in behind her to begin the festivities.

I was the only white guest there, except for a few dignitaries who had come to present her with several awards. Many friends, dignitaries, the Drum and Bugle Corps, elaborate decorations, and incredible assorted foods paid tribute to this well-loved icon of the Rose Bowl and Pasadena's history. After the food and awards presentation came the dancing. My foot was tapping to the rhythmic music, but I just couldn't get up the nerve to chime in. So I sat down with Robert and a few of his friends to chat while Dixie danced and partied with all of her good friends. What a send-off she had!

◆

After the Walkers moved to New Orleans, and as a direct result of Hurricane Katrina, they suffered the loss of nearly all of their belongings, including Robert's precious vinyls. I was able to send the boxes of tapes Robert had given me so he could retrieve some of the music he had lost in the flood. He has since returned them all, thanking me for being his backup. From time to time he checks in with me, letting me know how he and Dixie are getting along. I found that one of the downsides of this job was making good friends and then, all too quickly, having to move them away.

Considering my deep admiration for them both, I've often wondered if Mr. Walker was related to my childhood friend, Junior, who shared the same name—first and last—as well as an interest in sports. In any case, Mr. Walker, now of New Orleans, continues to serve as a reminder of my old childhood friend from San Diego.

WITH CLASSICS
9

Lying on the floor, I closed my eyes, and let the music take me to places reserved only for my imagination. It was late one Sunday afternoon at the tender age of fourteen that I discovered classical music while searching for my R&B station. Music had become a big part of my life by then, especially Rhythm and Blues. The sun had just started to go down, and I was home alone, with no plans for the evening, when I came upon the classical station quite by accident. Stravinsky's *Firebird Suite* was playing, and it quickly caught my attention. Previously, I had always related classical music to the movies. When a scene called for drama or tension of any sort, the early movies generally relied on the classics. I didn't know anything about the kind of music that set the mood for those films, but what I was hearing on the radio that day wasn't entirely unfamiliar to me.

As I started to pay closer attention to the music that I had accidentally tuned in, I was struck by the sensation of wandering through a quiet forest. As the room darkened, the music began to roll over me like an invisible wave, capturing me with its transitions of moods. I was hooked. From that day on, classical music was a valued part of my musical experience.

I WAS OUT OF MY TERRITORY, doing an appointment in Malibu for a saleswoman who had been called away on a family emergency. The house was secluded up in the hills and not easy to find. I wasn't even sure I was at the right address when I pulled into the driveway. Although there was no number posted, I took my chances and knocked on the door. The house looked to be a custom-built contemporary with the classic look of Mies van der Rohe, the architect famous for his clean lines and use of large flat planes of material.

When the door opened, a very stylish woman stood before me. I could see she belonged in this home. Her clothes and hair matched the style of the house; contemporary, yet tasteful.

"Hello, I'm Ron from the moving company," I said.

"Yes, please come in. I'm Doris Langley. We've been expecting you—or rather Gene, from your company."

I explained that Gene had been called out of town on a family emergency, and I was helping out with her territory.

"Have you heard the news lately?" I asked. "A fire has broken out just north of Pepperdine University."

"Oh my, no. I didn't know," Doris said.

She yelled out to her husband to turn on the radio for any news of the fire.

"I wondered why it looked a little foggier than usual this time of the year, but I guess it must be the smoke," she said.

"Let's hope the fire stays north of here. I couldn't help but notice your home is a classic."

"Are you familiar with Mies van der Rohe?"

"Yes very much so. I learned of Mies while studying design at Art Center, and I worked in the field for many years before I became an estimator. In fact, his name came to mind when I first pulled up to your home."

"Well then you would appreciate that the architect who designed this home was very influenced by Mies. We commissioned it to be built in 1988, and now we have to move. My husband has been offered the job of his dreams. He'll be playing with the Philadelphia Philharmonic in July. It's a great opportunity for him, and besides, he's burned out with the local Phil. I think they've used him up. He's very ready to move on."

"What instrument does he play?" I asked.

"Strings. You name, it he can play it. His main love is the cello. I play, as well, but only one instrument."

"And what would that be?"

"That beast over there in the corner. We're not going to be able to move it. We'll have to get a baby grand, I suspect."

I looked to the corner and saw what she meant.

"Do you play?" she asked.

"The piano is my favorite instrument. I wish I *could* play. But with the time it would take to get to a level I would approve of, I'd be an old man. I would rather listen to the pros I admire who've already put in the time."

"Well put. I understand how one can be put off with what it takes to get really good. I've studied from a very early age, and now its second nature for me."

I walked over to the beautiful grand piano, and touched its shiny rosewood surface. It was an incredible piece of craftsmanship. I secretly hoped that she would play for me, but I certainly didn't expect it.

"Come meet my husband," she said as I followed her through the house.

"Dear, this is Ron from the moving company. He's familiar with Mies van der Rohe, and he's a graduate of Art Center. Any news about the fire?"

"No dear," he said. "Just that they're worried about the winds, but so far, it's keeping well away from us."

Mr. Langley was seated at his desk, going over some papers. He looked up at me over his reading glasses and said, "I went to your Art Center. I always wanted to become a designer, but music won out, so here I am. What was your major?"

"Environmental design. It's funny. I always wanted to become a musician, and there I went into the design world."

"And now? What's become of your design world? Why are you doing this for a living?"

"I simply got overqualified, but I worked on some fascinating projects over my thirty years in the business."

Mr. and Mrs. Langley were very gracious, asking me all about my past career. They were impressed with the various projects on which I had worked. I told them how I came to love classical music, and they both said they'd had similar experiences.

When I told them that I had worked on the Queen Mary and met Jacques Cousteau, they said, in turn, that they had met him, as well, having played in the orchestra at the opening of the luxury liner museum.

"I was there at that opening!" I said excitedly.

"Well, what a coincidence," said Mr. Langley, warmly.

"I loved the piano solo that was played that evening," I said.

"That was Doris, my beautiful wife, who played that evening. You're in the presence of a great pianist," said Mr. Langley.

"I'm honored, but for the life of me, I can't remember the piece. It has haunted me all these years. I do remember I was very moved," I said.

"Honey, play a little for our new friend, would you please? We don't want Ron to be haunted any longer."

As Doris renewed my memories with that haunting, although long-forgotten melody called *La Boheme* (not from the opera), I sat with my eyes closed, taking it all in. Underscoring the music was the sound of sirens, getting louder and louder. The fire was closing in. We looked out of the window toward the north, and we could see the flames in the distance.
Then there was an announcement from a loudspeaker advising residents to prepare for evacuation. This was awful; this beautiful home, that beautiful piano, and no time.

"What do we do?" Doris said to her husband frantically.

"We do what the authorities say, my love."

"Please let me help you pack your cars with whatever you need to save," I said.

"No Ron, you should get out while you can," Mr. Langley said.

"I'm staying to help. I insist. With my car, we can save more of your belongings than we could otherwise," I said firmly.

The three of us began to pack the cars with paintings, papers, and all of the invaluable string instruments. Helicopters were flying over the house with their payload of water while loudspeaker announcements filled the air with the sound of panic. The smoke was becoming so thick we could hardly see the road as we each drove off the property. Fortunately, we found the blinking red lights of a fire truck on its way down the hill just ahead of us and followed it until the smoke began to clear. When we reached Pacific Coast Highway, there was chaos everywhere. We could see homes in flames above us.

The sky turned an ugly red, and black clouds of choking smoke surrounded us. The fire truck guided us south along the beach and found a way out of the danger. We pulled over and got out of our cars to look back at the disaster behind us. I felt a great sadness for the Langleys. Their beautiful home was in danger of being lost.

They weren't letting anyone back into the fire area that day, so I followed the Langleys to their friend's home in West LA, where I unloaded my car into their garage. After hugs all around, I went home to watch the news coverage of the fire.

I kept in touch with the Langley's by cell phone. The next day they were letting some residents back into the area, but not the Langleys. Their home was too remote, and there were too many hot spots lingering nearby. Three days went by until they were able to go back to what they hoped was still their home. Then I got the call.

"Ron, our home has been spared. We can't thank you enough for helping," Doris said.

"Hey, we music lovers must stick together. Besides if it was my home, I know you would have helped."

◆

Needless to say, the Langleys trusted my company to move them, and when they got settled in Philadelphia, they wrote me a letter thanking me again, inviting me to stay at their new home, and to come see them in concert. I was never able to take them up on their offer, but, over the years, I have enjoyed receiving their many cards and letters.

I felt both honored and torn by the loss of my new friends with whom I shared a love of classical music. Whenever I have a quiet moment, my mind drifts to that time when I helped save two classical musicians, so they could once again perform the music we all love so dearly.

FAME AND GENEROSITY
10

A trip to Canyon Country, a suburb of Los Angeles, found me driving up a long dirt road to a large ranch-style house surrounded by oak trees. The dust cloud that followed me up the road announced my arrival. On the front porch waited a woman, perhaps in her late sixties, wearing dungarees, a flannel shirt, and a large black cowboy hat. She reminded me of my aunt, who was always comfortable wearing one of her vast collection of cowboy hats, having fancied herself a cowgirl.

AS I GOT OUT OF MY CAR TO GREET HER, a barking golden retriever trotted up to me, wagging his tail. I petted the dog, while in the distance I heard the whinny of a horse.

"Good morning!" the woman shouted. "Don't worry about Buster. He'll just love you to death."

"I can see that. Good morning. Mrs. Jonas?" I closed the car door and began walking toward her, Buster at my heels.

"Yep, that's me. Come on in."

The interior of the house was built entirely of exposed timber. Overstuffed furniture filled the living room. The stairs that led to rooms above were flanked by a banister made of actual tree branches. The first few steps and rails looked like a tree that had risen out of the ground to support the entire stairway. Over the stone fireplace hung a vintage Winchester rifle. A large black iron kettle hovered in the hearth over a roaring fire. On the mantel above were artifacts straight out of the old West: a pistol, a sheriff's badge, a railroad watch, and even a wanted poster of the infamous Jesse James. Every table resembled the staircase, revealing someone's handiwork. Black iron lamps hung from the exposed-beam ceiling, adding authenticity to the rustic look and feel of the home.

"This house is wonderful!" I exclaimed. "I was in the design world before becoming an estimator, and I must say your home is the real thing. It truly looks and feels like a log cabin."

"Thank you. That's exactly what Mr. Jonas wanted. We built this house ourselves nearly thirty years ago. He made all the tables, you know."

"I'd like to shake your husband's hand for a job well done."

"You'll have to reach all the way to heaven. Sam died over three years ago. I've tried to run the ranch on my own, but it's getting too much for me now. Would you like me to show you around?"

"Yes, I'd like that very much."

"By the way, call me Kate," she said over her shoulder.

As I was given my tour, I conducted my inventory and found each room more charming than the next. Hand-made quilts on the beds and rope rugs in every room gave the home a warm, lived-in feel. Among the modern fixtures in the kitchen was an actual wood-burning stove with copper pots hung from a wagon wheel over the preparation island. On the counter sat a large porcelain cookie jar in the shape of a rooster. Several smaller vessels in the shape of farm animals served as containers for various condiments. The bathrooms were lined with wainscoting from the floor up to the towel rails. The walls were covered with dark green wallpaper with a field of small white flowers as though scattered across an open field. There were pedestal sinks and stand-alone bathtubs with Jacobean claw feet and shiny brass fixtures. In every room hung pictures and movie posters of the major cowboy heroes of the past. Among those prominently displayed was the Duke, himself— John Wayne.

Kate had excused herself for a moment, and I was left alone to finish the last room, which particularly caught my attention. Blue ribbons and plaques of odd names adorned the walls. Photos of rock stars were framed in gold, intermixed with a series of gold records. It was an odd collection of items that needed explanation.

After Kate returned, I was about to ask about the artifacts in the den when she suggested we see the exterior of her property. She led me out a side door and down to a small path that stretched to the next hillside. Buster led the way.

"This is all ours; forty-six acres of prime horse country," Kate said as she held her arms stretched out wide.

Large oak trees shaded the path as we made our way to various clearings where one beautiful horse after another was corralled by old style split rail fences. One by one, the horses came over to Kate and rubbed their heads against hers. She spoke to the horses as though they were old friends. They were magnificent.

It was a beautiful piece of property, a hidden oasis not forty miles from the big city. I mentioned how much my daughter loved horses and how she would ride any chance she got.

"Bring your daughter here, and she can ride any of my prize horses," Kate said.

I thanked her for the generous offer and asked what she meant by "prize horses." It turned out that the Jonas family raised thoroughbreds, and raced them all over the world.

"Any of your horses do well?" I asked.

" Oh, yes, we've won many races. You'll see when we get to the den."

The tour brought us to the tack house, where we found Buster waiting. On one wall were the bridles of eleven first-place winners, each with its name on a brass plaque mounted below.

"You know, my aunt would have loved to see all of this. She collected saddles, hoping one day to ride along the beach or off into the sunset. Every chance we got as a family we would bring her pictures of horses, whether they were on calendars or just photos from a magazine. I once got a stuffed toy pony from Wells Fargo as a promotional gift and, of course, it went right to my aunt. Porcelain horses of all sizes were displayed in her living room on shelves or on the table next to her favorite chair made of rawhide."

"Did she ever get to ride along the beach?"
"No, that dream of hers never happened. But for her memorial services, I created a slide show ending with a photo

of her fading back into a group of horses running along a beach, and giving her that last ride into the sunset."

"I wish I could have known her. She sounds like the real thing. A cowgirl at heart."

I smiled and nodded my head.

When we got back to the house, Kate began to explain the odd mixture of awards and accolades displayed on all four walls of the den. She told me of the various races her prize horses had won, and named them along with each of the jockeys perched atop the winners. On the back wall behind a large oversized desk were several gold records and many photos of a famous rock band of the '60s and early '70s. I learned that Kate managed the band that still made appearances, from time to time. The band's first guitar, displayed on the wall, had been given to Kate in appreciation of her efforts. Needless to say, I was blown away. But Kate seemed indifferent to her fame and success, and was ready to move on with her life.

"You can see this is a lot of work, with the horses and the music. I need to slow down. But one thing I can't live without is my wine."

"We can move your wine in special cartons that our company provides."

"Oh no. I'll move my wine myself. But I would need help moving my wine refrigerators."

Inside her garage she showed me three huge dual-zone wine refrigerators that held over fifty bottles each. "You can see these will need special care," she said.

After a quick call to my office, I was able to assure Mrs. Jonas that we had the special equipment to handle such items.

As I was finishing my survey, I thanked Kate again for inviting my daughter to ride one of her prize horses, although, unfortunately, we were unable to arrange my daughter's visit before the move.

Kate excused herself while I finished my paperwork, and when she returned, she presented me with two bottles of her best wine, which I later learned were worth a considerable amount of money. I promised that I would open them only on a special occasion, and that I would mention her name and her generosity.

As I drove back down the dirt road, with Buster running alongside of my car, I looked into my rearview mirror through the dust. There was Kate standing on her porch, waving her big black cowboy hat.

◆

When I think back to that day I'm reminded of my aunt, waving her cowboy hat as I drove away from her home in San Diego. On the anniversary of my aunt's passing I opened one of those bottles of wine, raising our glasses to both my aunt and Kate: two cowgirls who, one day, will meet riding along the beach off into the sunset.

I ALMOST MET SANDRA BULLOCK
11

There's something about Sandra Bullock. She has a playfulness about her, yet she can make a grown man dream. I've always been a fan of her comedic ways, and, through it all, I have often wondered what it would be like to actually know her. I can't explain my attraction to her other than that we would make the perfect couple, if only we were to meet. See what I mean about a grown man dreaming?

MY APPOINTMENT STARTED OFF IN THE MIDST OF CHAOS. I pulled up to a stately house in an old, high-end neighborhood of Los Angeles, and confusion surrounded me from the moment I entered the open door. I asked for the lady of the house, but no one seemed to know where she was, so I walked throughout the house calling her name.

"Mrs. Keller...Mrs. Keller?"

Eventually, I found her on her hands and knees, half inside a closet, going through boxes and yelling out to someone named Steven. I assumed Steven was her son after seeing what she was throwing out onto the floor.

"Steven, get in here and do something with your toys!" she shouted.

"Mrs. Keller?" I asked.

She turned and looked up at me with a questionable look. "Who are you?" she asked.

I was in the presence of a real beauty. When she got up, there stood a woman who must have been a model or at least a showgirl of some kind. She had long brown hair with a perfect complexion and penetrating dark eyes. Her smile could knock a grown man off his feet. Fortunately, I was holding steady.

"I'm here to do an estimate for your move; Ron, from the moving company," I said.

"Oh, sorry. Hi, yeah, it's me, Mrs. Keller. Call me Kathy," she said.

"What's going on here? It looks like you've started moving already," I said. A moving van was being loaded with furniture and boxes, and it seemed like there was no need for me.

"Oh, no, the truck out there is for our maid. She's got a friend to help her move and, besides, she needs to get to our new place first to set up. She'll actually be the one to do the coordinating. Our stuff still needs to be moved, and, between you and me, we want a reputable moving company. Keep that under your hat."

"Got it."

"I think you'd better know about our destination address. Are you available to go to the new house today?"

"Ah, yes. I have no other appointments after yours. Is there a problem at the new address?"

"It's up in the Hollywood Hills, off of a private—very narrow—road."

"Yeah, it would be helpful to see the destination. Sounds like we'll need to be sending our smaller trucks. They're called bobtails. What about access to the private road?" I asked.

"You've got to see it," she said

"Okay, when do we start?" I asked.

"We have to get this show on the road 'cause we've got a big party we're hosting this evening."

Just then the maid came into the room and said, "Miss Sandra Bullock is on the phone asking some questions about the party."

"I've got to get this. Be right back," she said.

When Kathy returned I asked, "You know Sandra Bullock?"

"My husband is a producer/director and we're kicking off a new movie tonight. And, yes, we know Sandra Bullock. There will be several people from the industry. Do you think you can finish your inventory by five tonight?"

"Sure, but we'd better get started if we're going to visit your new address."

We had to go to the new house first, according to Kathy, because she had a luncheon to attend. So we went off in her black Cadillac Escalade.

We wound up on the road to the crest of Mulholland Drive, passing opulent homes hidden away behind walls and gated private roadways. Kathy would point out various homes of celebrities as we passed.

"At the next bend, prepare to make a quick left onto a private road," Kathy said.

She stopped the SUV at the entrance leading to her property, and hopped out to unlock the gate. The house was adobe-style, with two archways that led to the front door, and windows set back under large wood beam overhangs. A gravel driveway looked like it could be a potential problem for the dollies, but not for the bobtails. As I took stock of the access, I lost sight of Kathy.

"Over here," she shouted from inside the front door. Once I caught up with her there, we took a quick tour of the house. Then Kathy said, "Come on. I want to show you our beautiful backyard."

Backyard, indeed. It was several acres of open space with large oak trees scattered about and an incredible view of the valley below. She told me the reason they were moving here was because they had three horses housed in a stable and wanted to have a place they could keep them nearby.

After seeing the property, which was an oasis right in the heart of the city, we came back inside and sat on the built-in bench at a large bay window overlooking the vast backyard. By now, we were getting along so well that the conversation started to take on a more personal tone.

"Were you in the biz?" I asked.

"I've been an actress of sorts, but no big roles or anything. I just couldn't cut it, so I became a wife and mom. I'm happy just being a part of the business through my husband."

"Has he got anything in theaters or TV I would have heard of?" I asked.

"He's more of an executive producer, the one who's behind the scenes."

She named several well-known movies, too many to mention. I then asked about Sandra Bullock, hinting that I would love to get an invitation to their party, although I knew it was next to impossible.

"I know everyone in Hollywood is writing a screenplay or a novel, and I guess I'm no different. Of course, mine is special," I said.

"Of course. What's it about?" she asked, indulging me.

"I'm a seventh generation Californian, and I'm writing a historical novel about my family's influence on the history of California. I'm hoping, one day, to see it on the big screen."

"Seventh generation? That's extremely rare. I don't think I've ever met anyone that goes so far back. Wait a minute, there's Javier our gardener, he says he goes way back to early California, but I'm sure not seven generations. I'll have to ask him. I know a little bit about the early Spanish soldiers who settled here. Many of them owned huge land grants. Was your family one of those land barons?"

"Actually they were. On my mother's side, the Arguello family, Santiago Arguello owned more land in California than anyone had before or has since. On my father's side, the Osuna family, owned 8,824 acres of prime horse country in San Diego, called Rancho San Dieguito. You might know it as Rancho Santa Fe."

"Wow. I know that property well. There's a lot of movie history related to that property. Many movie moguls in the '30s lived there and they even founded the Del Mar racetrack. Were you aware of that part of the history?"

"Yes. As a matter of fact, Bing Crosby lived on my ancestors' ranch and refurbished the original adobe my family owned and lived in. And I'm sure you know of Pickfair, the place where the 1984 Olympic equestrian venue was staged. They even used my family's branding iron design as one of their jumps.

"Mary Pickford and Douglas Fairbanks. The origin of the Pickfair name. I'll say 'wow' again! You *do* have quite a story to tell!" Kathy said, excitedly.

I continued telling my story, which seemed to garner genuine interest on the part of my captive audience of one.

"Hey, would you like to come to our party tonight? I'll even introduce you to Sandra Bullock."

"Are you serious?!"

"Yeah, why not. I think if you open up your pitch with your family ties to Rancho Santa Fe, they'll have to listen. It'll be a natural... And sure, I can introduce you to Sandy. She's very easy to know. No big."

"Is she involved with anyone? Not that I would have a chance in hell, but there's something about her... She's funny and sexy at the same time," I said.

"Yeah, I love her. She's one of my favorite people. You never know. This is Hollywood. Stranger things have happened. All you can do is ask. I'll talk to my husband about your story. Who knows? 'Sandra Bullock and the Moving Man.' It has a kind of ring to it," she said, making my heart race at the thought of two dreams coming true in one night.

"Wow. This is where I say it. This only happens in the movies. That would be fantastic. Thanks." I was hardly able to contain myself.

As we headed back to the house in LA, I continued to tell Kathy about my story and talked about the possibility of actually meeting Sandra Bullock. We had been away about an hour and-a-half, and, by then, it was time for Kathy's lunch. So I was left on my own to finish the inventory.

The house was huge. Every room was large, typical of the homes in the neighborhood. There were five bedrooms, maid's quarters, a game room, and even a projection room in the basement for screening movies. The master bedroom had a reading room the size of my small apartment. I finished in plenty of time to get back to my home and wait for the phone call to confirm my invitation to the party. The call never came. So I called Kathy and left a message, asking for feedback on the inventory and price quote that I had left. I was secretly hoping to hear about the party when she returned the call. I waited. No callback. There I was with all hopes dashed of meeting with an executive producer, let alone all the movie people who just might be persuaded to help me get my story onto the big screen. And, of course, there was Sandra Bullock.

◆

I was sure I would never hear from Mrs. Keller again.

Then, weeks later, she called and left a message on my work voice mail, apologizing for not getting back to me. It turned out that her husband had some people from the studios move them. And, apparently, the party I was hoping to attend went on as scheduled, Sandra Bullock and all. The only thing missing was me.

As dreams go, there went two right out the window.

DANCE I WILL
12

In her youth, my mother danced for the famed Loretta Young. She had always dreamed of being a professional dancer. Not until much later in her life did she dance again. At that point, square dancing became her passion. I guess it was her history of dance and her collection of Frank Sinatra records that inspired my own appreciation for song and dance, although I did not begin dancing until high school. At the time, we were doing a local dance called the "Choke" that was a take-off on the traditional West Coast swing dance style from the '40s.

The dances and music of the '30s and '40s are now a very essential part of my everyday life. At least once a week, sometimes twice, I'm on the dance floor performing a combination of East and West Coast swing.

Movies inspired my admiration of the professional dancer, like Fred Astaire, Ginger Rogers, Gene Kelly, Cyd Charisse, and Leslie Caron—to name a glorious few. I'm in awe of their ability to have glided across the floor with seemingly so little effort. When I dance now, it's as though I'm channeling their talents, as well as my mother's enthusiasm for dance. Watching these performers, absorbing everything they were doing with their bodies, made me feel as though I was a part of them, and motivated me to try to replicate what they did. Dancing is in my soul, and by watching these legendary professionals at work, I was made aware of the possibilities I could achieve with dedication and talent. Of course, in my advanced years, I don't ever expect to reach their level of perfection, but it's so much fun in the trying.

I find that dancing is the purest way to appreciate my early dancing role models, especially dancing to the great music of the big band era.

WITH THE RING OF A DOORBELL I found myself surrounded by the aura of one of my childhood heroines of dance, Leslie Caron. It wasn't her home but that of her managers and promoters: a husband-wife team. As we began to talk, they shared with me stories and memorabilia of the famous French-born dancer. I told them that I was a big fan and about how I had fantasized about her when I was just a boy. But, of course, back then, I had fantasized about a lot of glamorous movie stars.

Marilyn and Josh Breamish were moving out of Hollywood, going north, and getting out of the business. Ms. Caron was no longer dancing, but was now a judge on a television dance program. (This was long before *Dancing with the Stars*.) I was overwhelmed with the stories of this world-acclaimed actress, who was more than merely famous for me. She was my secret crush.

They had nothing but admiration and respect for Ms. Caron as they related stories of the famed ballet-trained actress.

"What was she like, I mean off-stage? You know, around the house—not acting…just being herself?"

"First of all she was French, and lived very much like a European in how she dressed, what she ate, and her mannerisms, in general. She was polite and gracious and made you feel you were in the presence of a lady," Mrs. Breamish said.

"And she never had any trouble with the suitors who came and went. Her smile had a sparkle to it that made many men melt," Mr. Breamish added

"Oh Josh, you know you had a crush on her, as well. We all knew it!" said Mrs. Breamish with a smirk.

"When I first saw *An American in Paris* I imagined I was dancing with her instead of that Gene Kelly guy. I guess my timing and talents were a little off," I said with a sigh.

"You know, she was very young when they shot that movie," Mrs. Breamish said

"I know. And I was even younger, so what was I thinking?"

"I'm guessing she's been married, but I don't know much about that. Does she have any children?" I asked.

"Well, it's common knowledge that she was married three times, all ending in divorce. She has two children from her second marriage and both of them are in the business, as well," said Mrs. Breamish.

My thoughts lingered again on my poor timing of having been born too late; in the US, not France; and being less than a world-class dancer...or whatever it was that could have won her heart. If only, given the right start, we would be happily married to this day, I thought. Talk about fantasy.

Mr. and Mrs. Breamish seemed happy to relive their Leslie Caron experiences with me. Ultimately, they left me with an autographed photo of her, which I treasure to this day.

◆

Not until, years later, did I see my screen idol in another movie, the French-produced, *Chocolat*. There she was, my childhood movie idol. I strained to see her in the scene where she and a few other women were peering through the multi-paned shop window at the chocolates on display. It felt just as it had the first time I saw her. I couldn't get enough of watching her.

If nothing else, it was an affirmation to know she was still around. Some things in life you just want never to see end. Sadly, my mother left us before she could see me dance. I'm sure she would have been my biggest fan. Before she died I was able to take her to two of Frank Sinatra's concerts. At the second concert my mother was in a wheelchair and we were put right up front, next to the stage. Later on, as we drove home, she told me, "Frank looked right at me while he sang *I've Got You Under My Skin*." She was in heaven.

Leslie Caron, where are you now?

BAD BOYS BAD DOG
13

I was a teenager in the early '50s in Highland Park, an area adjacent to Lincoln Heights, where several gangs vied for their territory. One of my friends, Alex, was a member of the Little Avenues, the younger version of The Avenues, which was a feared local gang. They all marked themselves with a tattooed cross on their hands, at the junction between the thumb and forefinger. The Little Avenues consisted of boys around thirteen to sixteen. Alex was big for his tender age of fourteen, and had the walk and the look of a bad boy, giving the illusion that he was confident and intimidating. He wore tan khaki trousers with the cuffs ironed a thin half inch, a white tee shirt, and the traditional leather jacket. His pointed-tip shoes were spit-polished black. His hair was worn in a ducktail, which, in those days, personified the look of cool.

This look was typical for many of the young boys attending Nightingale Junior High at the time. Just to blend in, they wore the uniform of the day, while keeping a healthy distance from gang activities. Alex would often come over to my house and say, "Come on. We're going to beat up some guys."
I would usually have some excuse, and pass on the invitation. After his little scuffle, he would come back to my house, and we would wrestle and roll around, and, even though he was a

lot bigger, I always got the better of him. Size wasn't everything.

Upon my graduation from Nightingale, my mother refused to let me attend Lincoln High School in Lincoln Heights. She said there was too much violence at that school, which there was. It was full of gang members from not only The Avenues, but also from gangs named Clover, Dog Town, Hazard, White Fence, and Cypress. So I went out of my district to Franklin High School, which was located in a much more conservative area of Highland Park. As a result, I lost all contact with my wrestling buddy, Alex.

MY NEXT APPOINTMENT FOUND ME BACK in the Lincoln Heights neighborhood from which my mother had banned me during high school. As I approached the old wood-frame house in dire need of repair and paint, the sound of a barking dog caught my attention. Dogs were always something to look out for when walking up to a strange house. Like the mailman, I had to be on my guard. When I knocked on the frame of the screen door, a small boy appeared, and just looked up at me, not saying a thing. In the background Spanish was being spoken, so in what little Spanish I knew, I said, "¿Dónde está tu madre?" ("Where is your Mother?")

The little boy ran back into the darkness of the room, and in a few minutes, a beautiful young woman came to the door, asking a question in Spanish that I couldn't understand.

Just then, from behind the young woman, a woman closer to my age smiled at me. "Are you here for the moving estimate?"

"Yes. My name is Ron and I'm from the moving company."

"It's free, no?"

"Yes, there is no charge for the estimate."

"*Bueno*, come in. My name is Jesse Chavez, and this is my niece, Loretta Fuentes. She does not speak English, so I will be her interpreter."

"Okay, yes. I was to meet with Mrs. Fuentes. She's moving to Mexico, I believe?"

"Oh yes, back to Calexico. She can't find a job here, and she misses her family so very much. I was trying to help her get started in the States, but she has given up and wants to go home. She also had a bad experience here, and she doesn't feel safe in such a big city."

"I'm sorry to hear that. It must be scary for a young woman, especially a very beautiful young lady, such as your niece, to find honest work here," I sympathized. "Did some one try to harm her?"

Chavez lowered her head and looked at me, squinting her eyes. "I'm glad she will not understand me when I tell you this. She was attacked by someone she was trying to get a job from."

"Did you call the police?"

"No, that is the problem. She is not a citizen, and she does not have a work permit, or anything. We were afraid to call the police."

"Still, you should report the incident, so it doesn't happen to anyone else."
"We took care of it, but I can't tell you anything more.".

For a second, I looked at Chavez with suspicion. I could tell she was hiding something from me, but I quickly looked away. Then I noticed on her left hand there was a tattoo of a cross; the sign of The Avenue gang. I realized there might have been some foul play, and I wasn't about to get any more involved than I already was. Then, Chavez started to ask me questions that led me right into a conversation that I should have avoided, but couldn't.

She noticed me looking at her hand and asked, "Did you grow up around here?"

I told her the story about my mother not letting me go to Lincoln High for fear of the gangs. She smirked and slowly nodded her head, as though she knew exactly what I was talking about.

"I noticed you looked at my tattoo. Do you know what it means?"

"One of the local gangs, maybe The Avenues?"

"Good guess. What made you say The Avenues?"

"It's the only gang I knew something about. I knew someone in the Little Avenues when I was a kid." There was an uncomfortable pause. "Those tattoos don't go away very easily, do they?"

"Hey, if you live in this neighborhood, it's a good thing to show who you are. It has helped me more times than I can count."

"Man, I know I shouldn't ask, but did it help with your niece?"

"Like I said, it's taken care of. That son-of-a-bitch won't be touching anyone else again."

I felt my skin crawl. I knew maybe a serious crime could have taken place, and now I was privy to that information. With a second look at Chavez, I envisioned her as having been a gang member in her youth. And it now looked as though she were still affiliated with the bad boys of LA.

I put my bag down on the sofa and took out only what I needed: my calculator and a tape measure. As I began my inventory with Chavez, I looked back and noticed that the little boy who had come to the door when I arrived had just opened my bag and pulled out my expensive equipment. Now, he was playing with it. I started to put things back in order while his mother, Mrs. Rodriguez, scolded him in Spanish. In the habit of carrying a small padlock for just such an occasion, I quickly used it to lock my bag. Still, I felt a little uncomfortable leaving my belongings to inquisitive little hands.

Only a few items were to be leaving with Miss Fuentes from the main house. So we made our way to the back house to complete the inventory. The dog I'd heard earlier was in the backyard behind a three-foot-high fence, and when I came into view, it started barking again. I had never heard a dog bark with such ferociousness. It sent cold chills down my spine to watch as the dog jumped at the gate, trying to get at me. As I approached, its growling and barking grew louder and louder. This had to be one of those killer dogs you hear about in the news that everyone fears, except that it was twice the size of any I had seen on TV. The dog was literally foaming at the mouth and determined to get over that fence. I was convinced I was about to become the victim of a vicious dog attack. My hands were sweating and my stomach began churning. I knew the dog could sense my fear, but I felt unable to control it.

"Are you sure that dog can't get over the fence?" I asked, almost trembling.

"Don't worry. As long as you're with me he won't bother you," Chavez explained.

"It doesn't seem that way, but if you say so, I'll try to relax," I said.

"He probably thinks we've brought him another victim," Chavez said with a smile.

"You bring him victims?" I asked.

"I'll bet when I said we took care of that guy who attacked my niece, you figured we cut him up, or even worse. No. We just introduced him to Bull. Scared the shit out of him. He won't be messing with any young girls again, not after that experience. Maybe you heard about that dog attack in the news last month. That was Bull. He didn't kill the jerk, just taught him a good lesson. That's why Bull wasn't put down. But, what does a dog know? He must think we're bringing him someone else to play with."

"Ah yeah, *play with*. Sounds like he did a little more than play with the guy."

"Hey, now that we've shared, you can call me Jesse, okay?"

"Sure, Jesse. When did you graduate from Lincoln?"

"You knew I went to Lincoln? I graduated in '58."
"That's when I graduated from Franklin. I wonder if you knew a couple of my friends from Nightingale who went there."

"Like who?"

"Al Fuentes and José Perez."

"Yeah, I knew José, but Al Fuentes jumped the fence and went to the other side. So I didn't have much to do with him after that."

"What do you mean, 'jumped the fence'?"

"He went over to the White Fence gang, and we actually had some issues with him. I mean our gang fought his gang. And, José, you know he became our school president. He was pretty cool. Everybody liked him. I didn't hang with him, but he was alright."

"Oh, and what about Alex Fonseca? Did you know him? He was one of my best friends back in junior high."

"Was he a big guy, and was he in the Little Avenues?"

"Yes, that's him. Did you know him?"

"No, he kept to himself, and then he disappeared. I don't remember seeing him at graduation."

I finished my inventory for Mrs. Rodriguez and referred her to our international carrier. Jesse put out the word to find Alex, and a year later, I got a call from my old wrestling buddy. He had joined the US Air Force and became an AP (Air Police.) We caught up on our good ol' days, and I told him about Jesse, the Avenues gang member. It was good to hook up with my buddy, whom I hadn't seen for all those years.

◆

The moving industry has rewarded me with so many unexpected memories of long-lost friends. I also never expected to see my old neighborhood again, which I discovered hadn't changed at all, except for a few new traffic signals and billboards. On the other hand, I found that, while I had moved on quite a long time before, time seemed to have stood still in Lincoln Heights. Even now, the old gangs are still there, only more violent.

LOFTY JOBS
14

I grew up in Los Angeles in the days when a 12-year-old boy could take the streetcar by himself downtown, and see two double features in a single day. I also got to watch the first high-rise being built at 7th and Figueroa. The Hilton hotel wasn't exactly a high rise, but it was just under the maximum allowed under the moratorium in place to build no higher than the city hall at thirteen stories.

I'm sure that my great-grandfather, one of L.A.'s first policemen—known as Keystone Cops back in the '20s—walked his beat among these very streets and buildings. Many old brick buildings from that era were still in use for offices and warehouses by the time I ventured downtown in the early '50s. Most of those early high-rises were concentrated in an area stretching from Alameda Street to the south and to Main Street to the north. Today, those same buildings have taken on a new role as loft living spaces and art studios. My next appointment was to take place in one of those loft apartments.

FINDING PARKING WAS A CHALLENGE, but once I'd pulled into a not-so-cheap lot, I was on my way. The street addresses to these old buildings were etched into the polished marble façades marking the entrance. This led to the elevator lobby, and, in most cases, to a reception desk.

These days the reception desks have turned into security counters manned by armed guards. I had to sign in and indicate the name of the resident I was visiting. The guard called my customer, and then gave me the okay. He directed me to a large steel door at the end of the hall that opened onto a loading dock.

There were four freight elevators that led up to the loft apartments, and I was to take the furthest one over. I lifted the large gray wooden gate and walked into a space so large you could drive a car into it. Once the gate was pulled down, I had to slide closed another set of gates on either side of the cab. When all was secured a loud bell rang, signaling me to select a floor from the oversized buttons on the cable box hanging from the ceiling. I pushed the number "8," and, after a slight shutter, the cab started to ascend.

Much to my surprise, the elevator opened right into the apartment I was seeking. I manually opened the gates, stepped into the loft area, and announced my presence. A woman appeared from behind a veil of sheer flowing material hung from the ceiling, which seemed to act as a room divider, separating the bed from the rest of the space. All four walls were made of exposed brick. The ductwork overhead was exposed, as well. Six large, double-hung windows looked out onto the city floor, keeping the noise at bay, and allowing an unfettered view of the San Gabriel Mountains to the north. The kitchen area was all stainless steel fixtures and very modern. To the right of the elevator door there was a retrofitted full bathroom with all the luxuries of a fine home. Various pieces of furniture were strategically placed around the space, breaking up the large area into separate uses. There was an eating area, a living room-like area, and what looked like a workout area with gym equipment and weights neatly arranged along one wall. The floor throughout was hardwood, with several rugs situated among the furniture arrangements.

"Hi. Ron from the moving company, I presume," she said.

"Yes, I made it. What an obstacle course," I said.

"We like it that way. I'm Sue Bradley. You're here to see Stewart Morris, right?"

Sue Bradley had short-cropped dark brown hair, much like a pageboy cut. Barefoot and wearing what looked like Japanese silk pajamas, Sue was pretty in a soft kind of way, but as soon as she spoke you could tell she was no pushover. Something about her told me that there was much more to this woman than met the eye.

"Yes, is he here?" I asked.

"He'll be here soon. I'm his better half, so I can get you started. Is this your first time in one of these lofts?"

"Yes." I looked around. "Pretty cool. You've made it quite livable. It's bigger than I expected," I said.

"We've got the whole floor. That's why the elevator brings you right to us."

"That doesn't seem very secure. How do you keep from getting unwanted visitors?"

"When you pushed the button to our floor, did you notice a slight hesitation before the elevator moved?"

"Yes, as a matter of fact. I just thought it was because it was old."

"That hesitation lets me see a photo of the visitor, so I know if it's friend or foe. Believe me, we're wired here for top security."

"What are you, the Feds or something?" I said jokingly.

"Yes," she said calmly. "As a matter of fact, my husband and I are federal agents, and this has been the ideal place for us while we're working in the LA area."

"My goodness, the real thing. Is there any protocol regarding security? Should we have unmarked vans?"

"No, that's not necessary. No one knows who we are. We keep a low profile, so no need for the cloak-and-dagger approach. We do have a form that the government requires any moving company to adhere to. So, should your company be chosen, that's the only type of security we would require. It's pretty standard stuff for moving any government official."

"So, are you being reassigned?"

"You could say that, but if I told you where, I'd have to kill you," she said in a slow, deliberate manner, barely smiling.

"Hopefully, not with your bare hands."

"I could, but I'd probably use a silencer on my .45."

Just then, I heard the elevator bell go off and wondered if she had company. I also heard what sounded like a Harley Davidson motorcycle. Sure enough, when the elevator arrived, a motorcycle pulled right into the apartment with a roar, then abruptly shut off, leaving my ears ringing to a deadly silence.

"And this is Stewart Morris," she said with her right arm stretched out in a bowing gesture. Hon, I've already told him too much, so I'm afraid we'll have to do him in. What do you think?"

I knew she was joking, but I was still feeling uneasy. Maybe because they *were* federal agents, and they probably *did* carry a gun or two.

"Hey babe, stop playing with the guy. He might take you seriously," Morris said.

Stewart Morris. The name sounded like that of a private detective from a 1940s radio program. But this guy was for real and so was his Sue Bradley. When Morris took off his helmet, his blond hair fell out and dropped onto his shoulders. His leather jacket was typical of those who ride the big bikes, but with no affiliation markings. From their appearance, this couple could have passed for your average Joe and Jane. Nothing like anyone might cast in an action movie. The one thing that made them ring true was their attention to detail. Every question I asked them was answered without hesitation, and in a more concise manner than any potential customer with whom I had ever dealt.

"Is everything going?" I asked.

"Yes," they said at once.

"We've made an inventory for you, It'll save you the time of doing it all over again," Bradley said.

"I'm sure you've done a proper job, but let's see if I can get close to what you've done, and we'll compare. What do you think?"

"Sounds good. We were just trying to save you some time."

"I have to enter it on my hand-held, anyway, so I can send it to my office via computer when I get home," I said.

"Hey honey, why don't we have one of those gadgets so we can just send messages to headquarters on our computer?" Bradley said.

"You know we can't send anything out there in the electronic world. We've got to stick to the old-fashioned secure way. Carrier pigeon," Morris said.

"Stewart made a funny. See, we're normal people. The only thing that sets us apart is that we have a license to carry automatic weapons," Bradley said.

I chuckled. "Yes, you're a little different from the norm."

"Do you want the Harley to go, as well?" I asked.

"Oh yes, and mine, too. It's in the shop, but it will be here by the time we need to move," Bradley said.

As I continued to survey the belongings of the Feds, we experienced a California tremor. It was a small earthquake, but it found a fault in the loft living environment. The only way out was the elevator, but the tremor had caused the doors to misalign. We were trapped.

"Our first earthquake. That wasn't so bad... *Now* what do we do?" Bradley asked.

Just then, we heard an announcement coming from the direction of the elevator. "This is the management. For your safety, please exit the building to the street using the fire escape. This is merely a precautionary measure. We will announce an all-clear after our inspection has completed." The announcement repeated; all the while, a fire bell was pulsating in the background.

"We've got alternatives, but we shouldn't bring our friend, Ron, into the know," Morris said, conspiratorially.

The Feds weren't the only thing that made this loft a stronghold of secrecy. It turned out that there was a secret escape staircase out of the loft. I waited while Morris and Bradley decided what to do with me.

"Come on, Ron, we'll be out of this place soon enough. No big deal if you know about our little escape secret. We'll use it instead of the fire escape, just for fun," Morris said, smiling, with a slight raising of his eyebrows.

It was right out of a James Bond movie. Morris activated some sort of lever near the kitchen sink that moved the refrigerator to one side, revealing a narrow steel staircase. It led out of the loft to a small landing. Then Morris presented a key to a locked door that brought us to the main corridor. I had a feeling they were just doing this for my benefit. But it was pretty cool, anyway. I could practically hear the *Mission: Impossible* theme as we made our way outside.

A few hours later, we returned to the apartment. But while maintenance fixed the elevator and inspected the building, I was treated to lunch at one of their downtown area hangouts. Bradley had put on some street clothes, looking like anyone one might wear downtown. I was introduced as one of their old friends, giving nothing away regarding their intended move.

As we walked back to their building, Morris said, "Well how did we do? Could you tell we were who we are?"

"I would never have guessed you were with the government. I'll bet the outside world perceives you two as a couple of yuppie bikers. You certainly acted the part. I was very impressed."

"That's how we live our lives until we have to get serious. But, for now, we're on a break. Like I said earlier, you know too much, but how do you know we've told you anything we haven't cleared with our superiors? Anyway, not to worry; I think we can trust you. Besides we know where you work," said Bradley, grinning.

◆

The move was set, and no one in my company knew the couple being moved was federal agents. I was to keep that part to myself, and I have, until now. But that was many years ago, and I'm sure there's been no loss of national security in the interim.

It was the first and last time I moved such high profile customers; ones who legally packed guns, anyway. Somewhere in the back of my mind I am still unconvinced whether they were the real thing or just putting me on.

Whenever I drive through that older section of downtown LA, I'm reminded of my great-grandfather. The colorful cop was quite a character. At the start of his law enforcement career, he would direct traffic standing on a box in the middle of an intersection between those old buildings. Among the stories

I've heard was that he was known for putting on quite a show, wiggling his behind and doing a little dance for the passersby. After a thirty-year stint, he retired from the force as a captain. His badge still remains with the family as a relic of old downtown Los Angeles and its law enforcement history

COLD FISH AND OYSTERS
15

I had only been on the job for a few months, and was still a little unsteady on my feet. Because I was new, they kept my appointments to a minimum so I could get the hang of walking up to a stranger's home and asking them for their business. One of the more seasoned salesmen told me it had always been his fantasy to have a beautiful woman answer the door in a flimsy negligee. I, of course, put that right out of my head, but one could hope.

WHEN THE DOOR OPENED, there stood a woman with her claws out and a squint in her eye. She already had an attitude. I found myself poised for a battle with this cold fish wearing no make-up and hair pulled back tight against her head. Sheila Whitcom was impatient with my questions and gave short, to-the-point answers.

"How long will this take? I've got some important things to attend to," she said firmly.

"Not long. Forty-five minutes to an hour at most," I answered.

"That's too long. Can you hurry it up a bit?"

"Sure..." I said, not wanting to have to spend any more time than necessary at this appointment. "How long have you lived in this house?"

"What does that have to do with the move?"

"It helps to know how much trauma you might be experiencing so I can treat the interview appropriately."

"Oh. I see." She softened her tone a bit. "I guess I'm a little stressed. I hate moving."

"I wouldn't want to move at this time in my life."

"What do you mean, this time in your life?"

"I've got two children who live locally and all my good friends live here in the LA area."

"All I've got here is my mother, and I'll eventually move her up to Sacramento to live with me. The rest of my family and friends are back east, so no big deal. But I still hate moving."

As I continued with my interview, her negative demeanor started to weaken. She would actually smile from time to time. A nice smile that seemed to wash away that first cold impression she had displayed. Whether it was my charming personality or her feeling more comfortable with the process, she began to come around. By the time we got to the backyard, we were actually laughing.

"Are you going to miss my city?" I asked.

"Your city. What makes this *your* city?"

"I'll have you know I'm a member of three of the eleven founding families of Los Angeles. You're speaking with California royalty," I boasted.

"And what would you want from me, your Lordship?" she said with a smile.

"Sign on the dotted line, and walk with me into the sunset," I said.

My playful flirtation was as much a surprise to me as it was to her. She looked at me with new interest, showing a curious smile. We started to connect in more ways than one. Something else was stirring, and we both felt it.

Back to the house. We entered the master bedroom to finish the inventory, and the tension was such that we both began to fidget, especially with her big king-size bed before us. I can't explain how it happened, but we found ourselves extremely attracted to each other. This cold fish turned out to be the catch of the day.

After leaving her, I found myself calling her and carrying on long conversations, not only about her upcoming move. We talked for hours over the next few days, and with each conversation I felt that she was getting to know me on a deeper level than I thought possible.

Her work environment consisted mostly of male lawyers who usually had something shallow or demeaning to say to her. She said that she found me to be a gentleman, and much more interesting than any of her coworkers or the men she had dated in the past. Sheila was feeding my ego like no other. With each conversation she would come up with a new compliment. She began to know me as well as I knew myself. It was incredible.

The following week, Sheila invited me to her home. When the door opened this time, there stood an entirely different person. There was no negligee, but nothing else was missing. The make-up was on, her hair was down, and an alluring smile was there to greet me. Walking in, the first thing I noticed along with an assortment of munchies was a bowl of oysters sitting on the counter.

"Have some oysters," she said with a smile.

"No thanks. I'm not a big fan," I said with a bit of a frown.

She guided me to the sofa where we sat and talked for a short time. Then the fireworks began. We could hardly control our passions, but somehow found ourselves taking deep breaths, trying to make sense of how quickly this was getting out of control. Looking into each other's eyes, she managed to break the tension with some humor.

"It's a good thing you refused the oysters," she said gasping for breath.

"Is it a good thing? Maybe I'll have just one."

"I don't think you need even one. Can we talk some more?"

We got back to learning more about each other, finding that talking took precedence over a physical encounter at this time. This was getting serious fast. We continued to talk into the night and set a date to go dancing the following weekend.

On the dance floor, we whirled around to the fast music as though we had been dancing together all of our lives. When the music slowed down we were clinging to each other like long-lost lovers. Over the next several days, our phone conversations consisted of each trying to convince the other to move or to stay. Sheila needed to relocate to Sacramento to be an assistant to the Attorney General at the State Capitol. I, on the other hand, hoped to convince Sheila to stay in the area, because I wasn't ready to leave friends and family.

After many attempts to resolve the issue, we were at a stalemate. Neither could convince the other. Much to my dismay, Sheila finally made her decision to go with her original plans. I tried to make contact with her after her decision, but she refused to answer my phone calls. Finally, I showed up on her doorstep to confront her. She opened the door, crying. Her make-up was smeared, her hair mussed, as she began to speak. "It's been too painful to speak with you. Please, let's part friends. Can we?" she sobbed.

◆

It wasn't a flimsy negligee at the door, but much more. It was love unexpected. It took quite a while for me to get over that whirlwind romance and to stop hoping the next door that opened would reveal more of the same.

I had found someone beyond my expectations, more wonderful than I could possibly imagine—and, just as suddenly, she was taken away. Sheila moved to Sacramento, and despite many failed attempts to contact her, I was never to hear from her again.

VAN GOGH
16

When I walked into the hallowed halls of Art Center and saw the student work displayed on the walls, I said to myself, *if they can make me this good, I'm enrolling right away*! Well, it took a full year for me to gather enough of a portfolio to qualify for entrance into this prestigious design college. After graduating, I had a thirty-year career in the design world, and I even taught my craft at a couple of colleges. Once in a while, my appointments led me to struggling young artists on their way up. And up I went on this day, to glimpse the future of art.

I CLIMBED THE 127 STEPS leading to a small house at the top of the hill in the Silverlake district of Los Angeles where artists and performers make their home. Almost out of breath, I knocked on the door. A young lady dressed in what looked like hand-me-down clothes from a thrift shop opened the door, smiling.

"Ron?"

"Yes."

"I'm Patty Moran. Come in. Would you like a glass of water?"

"Yes, thank you."

It happened to be a very hot day, and the water was a welcome treat especially after my long hike up the stairs. As Patty ran off to the kitchen to get the water, I found myself surrounded by art. Colorful and strange images filled the walls. Statuary of an indeterminate nature was mounted on orange crates and makeshift pedestals. The ceiling was painted flat black with a winged devil-like creature staring down at me.

"Would you like ice?"

"No, just bottled water would be fine."

"Not in my home. I filter my water from the tap. It's better than bottled."

"Great. That'll be fine. Looks like I came to the home of an artist."

"Well, I'm an artist in training. My day job pays the bills."

"What's your day job?"

"I'm an RN. I work in the emergency O.R. at Scripps Hospital in San Diego."

"Is that why you're moving south? Did you just land the job?"

"No. I've been commuting for the last two years. I've been working only three days a week, so I come back here to stay in touch with my creative side. My job is pretty stressful, and I needed the change, but the commute is starting to be too expensive. I'm here Friday through Monday, so it has worked out, but now it's time. Besides, I'll be working five days a week soon.,"

"I wouldn't have guessed your occupation from the style of art you do, but I can say it is well done. My job before becoming an estimator was in a related field, and I taught at a few colleges."

"Really, what did you teach?"

"Lettering and design, the more commercial side of art. But I can appreciate good work when I see it."

"Did you notice my Van Gogh portrait in the dining room? It's that small piece just over there next to the window."

"No I missed that."

I walked over to where Patty pointed, and was amazed at the detail.

"This is quite good, such consistent fine lines. You must have used a triple "O" brush."

"Look closer."

I got about four inches away from the piece, and squinted my eyes to appreciate the technique. "Looks a little…dimensional. How did you do that?"

"Well you know Van Gogh had red hair and I have red hair…so I used my hair to create the piece…it's my pubic hair."

I immediately bolted back with my eyes popping from my head, my mouth agape. I took a quick glance at Patty, then back to the piece again, squinting to see the detail. Sure enough, there was an unmistakable curl to the lines. "This is incredible," I stammered.

But, it *was* incredible. Making my way back down the steps I kept trying to imagine just how she did it.

◆

Once again, I had found a budding artist who surprised me with a talent that was off the charts. Patty had made me realize how out of touch I was with the current art world. Years later, I visited my alma mater with a couple of friends who had attended Art Center back in the sixties. There we were, three older guys, touring the gallery of student work, scratching our heads. Very much like Patty's work, there were art pieces we just couldn't quite understand. The art world had moved on, leaving us alumni in the dust.

HOT AND SPICY
17

What American doesn't like Chinese food? From an early age, I had American-style chow mein served at home while living with my aunt and uncle in San Diego. When my mother remarried we returned to Los Angeles, where I had been born, and at least one night a week we would go out for a Chinese dinner at The Dragon Pearl in Highland Park. One of my best friends took a Chinese cooking class at UCLA, and when the instructor asked if anyone wanted to go to China, the entire class responded. Mark came back from that experience knowing more about the art of Chinese cooking than anyone I knew. He would invite me to meet him in Chinatown for dinner at the Golden Dragon, and when the waiter came, he ordered directly from the kitchen without even looking at the menu, and every dish was outstanding.

MY NEXT APPOINTMENT WAS in the predominately Chinese neighborhood of San Gabriel, a suburb of Los Angeles.

The apartment complex directory showed at least seven residents named Wong. I was looking for Charles Wong, but there were three names listed as "C. Wong," so it was hit-and-miss until I found the right one.

"Hello," I heard from the intercom. A woman with a very strong accent asked me who was calling. I had to tell her several times before she was able to understand me. This was going to be a challenge.

"I'm here to do an estimate for your move. Is this the home of Charles Wong?" I asked.

"Yes. This is Mrs. Charles Wong. Please come up to apartment 222," she said.

Mrs. Wong greeted me with a smile and a bow as I entered her home. "You are Lon, right, to move my husband?" she asked.

"Yes, I'm Ron from the moving company," I replied.

"Oh, forgive me. I maybe pronounce your name incorrectly. I apologize." Again she bowed her head. "I'm only recently here in your country from Hong Kong. My husband had to go San Francisco on business, and he will have me do the business with you," she said.

"You have a very nice apartment here," I said.

The apartment definitely had a Chinese theme. The first thing staring me in the face, as I entered, was a huge dragon relief made of polished gold-like metal set against a bright red wall. Two large stone lions guarded the fireplace. The furniture, which consisted of one sofa and two armchairs, was covered in black leather upholstery. The thick shag carpet was also black. A seven-foot silk Chinese elm tree stood in one corner of the room. Above, in a split-level, was the dining area. The dining table and hutch were a high gloss black lacquer.

The backs and seats of the chairs were covered with a red fabric with some sort of Chinese symbol woven in gold.

"Oh, this is not my apartment. It is my husband's apartment. His business provides it for him when he comes to America. I am only here for the first time in your country two days ago," she said.

"Welcome to America," I said with a bow.

"Thank you. It's a very strange place, your America. I expected to see many Americans, but I only see Chinese people. Very strange."

"Well, maybe your husband didn't explain, but this particular part of Los Angeles has many Chinese residents. I remember when it was all Mexican families," I said.

"Where did the Mexicans go?"

"I don't really know. I believe many moved east."

"To China?" Mrs. Wong asked surprised.

"No, I meant East Los Angeles."

"Oh, forgive me. I made a mistake," she apologized. "Have you ever been to China?"

"No, but I love Chinese food," I said with a smile.

Mrs. Wong seemed very surprised when I said I loved Chinese food, and that kind of threw me.

"You eat Chinese food? And you say you love it. Very strange. You are an American. I thought Americans only eat hamburgers and fried potatoes!"

"Americans like all kinds of food, not just hamburgers and fries. We like Italian food, Mexican food, French food, and yes, Chinese food, too. In fact, I only have one friend who doesn't like Chinese food, and he eats a lot of meat and potatoes."

"Where do you get your Chinese food?"

"There are many good Chinese restaurants here in the City."

"Have you ever had homemade Chinese food?"

"No. Oh, wait a minute. My aunt prepared American-style chow mein. I don't think it was the real thing."

"I think I should make you some real homemade Chinese food, and then you will know what real Chinese food should taste like. Would you like that?"

"Yes, I think I would, but when? I don't want to inconvenience you. You must be very busy."

"When we come back from the shop, we will see how much time is left."

"The shop?"

"We have to go to Chinatown to the shop so you can see what my husband wants moved."

"Oh, so nothing from the apartment is to be moved?"

It turned out that the apartment provided for Mr. Wong came completely furnished, dragon and all, so off we went to the shop in Chinatown. I hadn't planned on this trip, so it was a good thing there weren't any other appointments scheduled for that day. When we arrived, I was introduced to Lu Chang, the shop owner. He led us down to the basement where I found a huge collection of artifacts stored from floor to ceiling. Filling the basement were large stone lions, bronze warriors from a long-past dynasty, foo dog statuaries, ceremonial porcelain horses, and a variety of Buddha heads. All but a few of these items were to be moved. Doing the inventory turned out to be a monumental task. We were there for two and-a-half hours, and I wasn't even sure I got it all.

"I think I'd better come back tomorrow to make sure of my count. It's getting late, and looks like the shop is closing," I said to Mrs. Wong.

"I didn't realize there were so many pieces. So sorry."

"It's okay. Bigger job, more money. It is a good thing," I said smiling.

"There's no time to cook for you, so I will take you to a good Chinese dinner right here in Chinatown. Do you have time?"

We found ourselves at the Golden Dragon, the same place that Mark and I used to go. When the waiter came, Mrs. Wong said to me. "Do you know what you want?"

"I'll leave it up to you to order. Just make it hot and spicy."

"Are you sure you want it hot and spicy?" Mrs. Wong was surprised.

"Yes, the hotter the better."

"Very strange. Are you very sure you can handle the hot and spicy Chinese food?"

"Yes, I'm sure. And I will eat with chopsticks, as well."

"Oh my. This is very strange. Are you sure you are not Chinese?"

We laughed at her little joke. Then Mrs. Wong ordered from the kitchen, just like my friend Mark would do. Interestingly, she ordered almost the same dishes, so I was ready to impress Mrs. Wong by eating everything she ordered. And I did. We were getting along so well, talking about personal things. I asked her how long her husband stayed away from home when he came to America, and if she had any children. In return, she asked me about my family life, and why I wasn't with a woman, especially a Chinese woman. I think we were relating on a much closer level that I had expected.

"Have you ever had a Chinese girlfriend?"

"I dated a Chinese girl once. If you'd like, I will tell you a story about her and about something she said, and I would ask you if there is any truth to what she told me."

"Please go ahead."

"This young lady was very shy and reserved, so I tried to be a gentleman and not be too aggressive with her on our date. But, she surprised me with a comment that later took our relationship to a new level. I guess I'm wondering if this is a typical feeling among Chinese women."

"What did she say, what did she say?"

"She said that Chinese women are very cold and reserved on the outside but that inside they are a raging fire."

I waited for a comment, but suddenly realized I might have stepped over the line. Hoping I hadn't offended Mrs. Wong, I sat in silence.

"Ron, I must be honest with you. What your young Chinese lady said to you is absolutely the truth. Chinese girls are told at a very young age to be reserved, but we are indeed hot and spicy inside," she said, blushing slightly.

As I walked away from her apartment, readying myself for the next day, I was hoping and praying Mrs. Wong would keep our little hot and spicy stories to herself.

The next day we returned to the shop to finish the inventory and to say our goodbyes. Mrs. Wong was going to be visiting some family members in San Diego. When I met with Mr. Wong upon his return to LA two days later, he was pleased with the estimate, and agreed to hire my company to do his move. It took two vans filled to capacity and special heavy equipment to move many of the heavy pieces from the shop's basement.

◆

The experience with Mrs. Wong opened my eyes to a culture of which I knew little. I still believe she was a fair representative of the graciousness of the women of China. Speaking with this lady of the East also gave me an insight into the innermost passions they so effectively kept under wraps

THE COLLECTOR
18

I've run across many customers who like to share their odd and not-so-odd collections. A few are very serious about their treasures, having received media recognition for their efforts. Others simply got started collecting and never stopped. Although some might be called hoarders I wouldn't qualify for the term. I'm only guilty of collecting things that no one else would consider important enough.

The most infamous such customer was Mrs. Dunbar, who collected Garfield the Cat. I mean, she collected Garfield in a big way. There was nothing in her home that wasn't some form of Garfield. I never would have guessed that I could learn something from someone like her, but I did.

AS YOU FIRST ENTERED HER HOME, a larger than life stuffed Garfield The Cat greeted you at the door. Even the doorbell was a replica of the famous cartoon cat's nose. Once in the house, you would check under your feet. Yes, you were walking on a fluffy image of the famous cat. There were also stuffed Garfields displayed on a shelf that spanned the perimeter of the room. The walls were painted with murals of the famous feline and there were display cabinets holding every conceivable notion of the animated character. Glued to the ceiling, from wall to wall were paper cutouts of Garfield. As you entered the dining room, the first thing you saw was a dining table with legs in the form of Garfield statuettes. The door to the kitchen was designed as an open mouth of the hungry cat. Kitchen utensils, dishes, pots and pans all reminded you of where you were. In the bedrooms, you guessed it: Garfield bedspreads, pillows, and curtains.

The toilet seat covers, the towels, the hamper, and even the toothbrush had the likeness of the famous cartoon cat. Mrs. Dunbar had specially made ceramic tiles for the floor of the bathroom and the kitchen. Everywhere I looked, there was the cat. Even inside the closets, there was Garfield leering at me. He was either hanging on the rack as clothing or sitting on the floor as furry yellow slippers with those big oval, unblinking eyes. Then, a walk into the yard to find topiaries shaped like you-know-who. Finally, relief, or so I thought. The swimming pool was an ordinary rectangle. But on closer inspection I was not surprised to spot a watery image of Garfield looking up at me from the bottom of the pool.

"How did you get started with this collection?" I asked.

"My granddaughter fell in love with Garfield when she was about three, so like a good grandmother I would seek out anything having to do with the character. After being flooded with Garfield stuff for a few years, she seemed to have grown tired of the big yellow cat and moved on to other toys. On her seventh birthday, as I was about to hand her yet another Garfield find, she asked me, 'Grandma would you take care of all my Garfield things, so when I grow up I can give them to my daughter?' Well that came as a jolt and I pulled back the gift I was about to hand her. Then, I said, 'this will be the last Garfield I give you. Take it, and I'll keep all the rest for you safe at my home. Would that be okay?' Afterward my daughter told me that a rich neighbor friend of my granddaughter had a huge collection of Garfield, and she just didn't want to compete with her. It's a good thing I hadn't known about the neighbor or I would have gone broke trying to keep her collection ahead of her friend's."

"Okay, that explains it. But that collection couldn't have been near the volume you have here today. Just curious. Has your granddaughter ever asked about it?"

"My granddaughter is now twenty-seven, and after she had her first child she pleaded with me not to start her daughter on the yellow cat. But by then, I was already hooked. I guess I thought through the years I would pass up that rich neighbor of hers by sheer attrition. But look what's happened. I've become obsessed with the collection, myself. I guess the little bit of fame that came along with my compulsion was addictive. I just couldn't stop. Now I'm too old to keep this up any longer. I'm eighty-five, you know. Besides, Garfield is getting harder to find, and I'm thinking of unloading it all on someone. Problem is, I really don't know who or even how to get started."

"I would have never guessed you to be eighty-five. You don't look or sound like an eighty-five year old, at all."

"Oh, you're very kind. Thank you for the compliment. I suppose my passion for this collection had something to do with staying young at heart. But I'm slowing down, and I think it's time to act my age."

Cloris Dunbar had won several awards for her compulsion and gave me the rundown on each and every one of them. It was a challenge to get an accurate survey of the varied items in her special collection. Nevertheless, it was an unexpected treat to see the extraordinary instead of the ordinary, and especially to meet someone whose passion kept her youthful in spirit.

After spending two hours doing the survey, Mrs. Dunbar confessed to me that she really wasn't moving but wanted an accurate account of her collection so she could maybe sell or donate her collections one day. With that, she took two hours of my life that I'll never get back. When I was finished, she turned to me and smiled, then rewarded me with one of her stuffed trinkets.

I thanked Mrs. Dunbar, and wished her well with her plan to step back from her long-held passion. But I reminded her that she might want to take up another hobby to keep the fire of youth burning.

◆

My own collections consist of items or things I think I can't do without. "I'll have a need for this one day" Is my reasoning. And sure enough those days have actually been there when I would ask myself, *I know I have one of those, but where in the hell is it?*

The lesson I learned from Mrs. Dunbar was to get rid of those things "I might need one day" and not waste time looking for them. Even more important is to not leave these useless items for my family to deal with after I'm gone. I was overwhelmed with the Garfield collection and how Mrs. Dunbar went overboard with her compulsion. Time to clean up my act.

I think the most important thing I learned from Mrs. Dunbar was that having a passion for something keeps your mind sharp. So when I reach the ripe old age of eighty-five, hopefully I'll still have my wits about me, like the youthful collector of Garfield the Cat.

ROCKIN' ROCKET
19

I grew up on a steady diet of rock and roll, and on this day I was to meet someone who took his music very seriously. It never ceases to amaze me, though, just when I think I've got my customers all figured out, they take off in a whole new direction.

I WALKED UP TO AN UNASSUMING APARTMENT, AND KNOCKED. A young woman answered and looked puzzled to see me. She appeared to be about twenty-two or twenty-three, but not much more. On second look, she could have been a teenager.

"I'm from the moving company to do an estimate. Is Jon Stevenson here?"

She smiled and scampered off in her bare feet, disappearing through a beaded doorway. I didn't know what to make of it at first but when she came back, she started to sign, and then gestured to me that she that she was deaf. I once knew someone who became deaf after a botched operation and communicated with her by learning how to sign myself. So I let the young lady know that I understood. She told me that Jon would be with me in a moment.

The apartment was dark and in need of a good clean-up. Clothes were strung about, and there were magazines stacked in every unoccupied corner of the room. Tie-dye fabric covered the sofa, and the young lady who answered the door looked like a misplaced flower child wearing a similar-looking tie-dye skirt. A questionable smoking apparatus was on the coffee table, surrounded by ashes from incense sticks, one of which was billowing its sweet smoke into the room. A black cat lay across the back of the sofa, sound asleep. From the other room rock music was blasting with the distinct sound of the sixties. Then, suddenly, it stopped. From behind the beaded doorway came a tall bearded man with long gray hair. As soon as he saw me his eyes lit up as though he were looking at a long-lost friend. He greeted me with a smile, and both arms outstretched.

"Hey man, welcome to my home. Ron, right?"

"Yes," I said. "Jon Stevenson?"

"Yeah. Just call me Jon. Have a seat." He gestured to the girl, whose name was Jenny. "Make some room for our guest."

Jenny quickly moved some clothes off a chair, then stepped back and stood there like an obedient servant. I sat down and began to ask my usual questions about what was going and what was staying. But I was interrupted.

"Would you like some herbal tea?" Jon asked.

"Sure. Sounds good."

"Jenny, bring us some tea and some of those great cookies you baked. And some dried fruit," Jon said.

I was about to have a hippie snack. I only hoped the cookies weren't laced with anything.

Jon's mood seemed to shift. He looked at me with a scowl on his face, his fists clenched. "So, what's it like going into strangers' homes and asking for their money?"

I sensed some hostility, so my gut feeling was to squelch this stance, and quick. "Take a look at my card just under my name. You see what it reads? *Moving Counselor*. When I took this job I hated the idea of being called a salesman, so when my next batch of cards came out I gave myself that title. I truly feel that's what I do. I've done this now for about eight months and I've experienced how unsettling it is to move. Asking for money is the hardest part of my job but I feel much better about it when I know I've made someone's moving experience a positive one."

"Hey, man, maybe I stepped out of line when I said that thing about asking for money. Sorry about that. I see now what you mean about the helping thing. That's cool. You're alright."

As I looked into his eyes, I noticed another shift in his manner. His voice became calmer and he relaxed his clenched fists.

Jenny came with the tea and treats. She had put a lot of effort into the arrangement of cookies and dried fruit. I was impressed, and mentioned that it looked very artistic.

"I'm putting Jenny through art school, and now everything she touches displays her talents," Jon said.

He motioned to Jenny to bring out some of her art to show me. She seemed shy at first, but he insisted. So she finally smiled, backed up a few steps, paused, and then, like a ballet dancer, floated out of the room with the grace of a swan.

"I've got her in a very good school, where I'm sure she will do well," Jon said.

"What school?" I asked.

"The Art Center. Have you heard of it?" Jon asked.

"I graduated from Art Center several years ago," I said excitedly.

"Cool. Maybe you can let her know if she's progressing well. But let's not tell her just yet that you went to her school."

Jenny came into the living room with her portfolio and proceeded to show me her art work one at a time. Jon looked over at me, raising his eyebrows. He seemed to be asking for approval.

Her work was good. It still needed a little improvement but definitely had promise. She was only in her second semester, so most of the assignments were, from what I could remember, simple, and without much opportunity to exercise creativity. But her craftsmanship was exceptional.

Then she pulled out pieces that were obviously not assignments from school. They were abstract paintings of what looked like solar systems. Each painting was more spectacular than the next. It turned out that these efforts are what got her into Art Center.

"Wow, you're very talented," I signed to her. "You have quite a gift. I hope you continue pursuing your passion!"

"Ron here is a graduate of the Art Center," Jon signed to Jenny, as he spoke aloud.

Jenny's face started turning a bright red.

I pointed out to her that her craftsmanship was very good and to keep working in the direction of the work she had done prior to Art Center.

"What inspired your pieces of outer space?" I asked Jenny, speaking very deliberately and slowly so she could read my lips.

Jenny smiled then turned her head, and pointed to Jon.

"We'll get to that a little later. Shall we get started?" Jon asked.

As we went through the apartment, our final stop was the source of the music I had heard earlier. The room was filled with sound equipment. A large sound mixer along with speakers and racks of CDs took every square inch of the room.

"Is this what you do for a living?" I asked.

"No. I'm a rocket scientist," Jon said.

I chuckled and said. "Sure…a rocket scientist."

"No. I really am a rocket scientist at JPL. The music mixing is just a hobby."

I was blown away, and now understood where Jenny got the inspiration for her art pieces.

"What projects have you worked on?"

Jon told me of the moon landings and satellite launches with which he was involved.

◆

I now had a new respect for Jon, knowing I was in the presence of an American icon, who had helped bring the unknown into our lives on our insignificant Third Rock from the Sun. And I was impressed with Jenny, who had an obvious future in the arts. I also liked the fact that, by the end of our meeting, Jon was able to see me as an honest and worthy professional who could provide constructive criticism and encouragement to Jenny's efforts. It seemed we had both jumped to conclusions about each other before letting our meeting play out to its finale.

ALL IN BLACK
20

We've all had our dealings with car salesmen. Well, if there were a cake to be taken, this is the one who took it. It's not so much that it was a car salesman I was visiting that caught me off-guard, but how he and his wife spent their alone time.

I pulled up to a large, pretentious home on the outskirts of Los Angeles in an area called Canyon Country. Many of the homes in this particular neighborhood were oversized for the lots they were squeezed onto. These mini-mansions were better suited for a half-acre lot.

AFTER RINGING THE DOORBELL I STEPPED BACK from the oversized double doors, and waited. The footsteps I heard sounded like tap dancing on a marble floor. Then muffled voices, one louder than the other, then silence. The door opened. There stood a middle-aged man with a large belly dressed all in black. His hair was slicked back tight against his balding head, with silver streaks of grey peppered within what once had been a crop of black hair.

"From the moving company, yes?" He questioned.

"Yes, Ron. Mr. Gabrielli?" I asked.

"Yes, yes, come in. How are you this fine day?" he asked, his smiling stretching from ear to ear. The man had "salesman" written all across his face.

"Just another beautiful day in Southern California," I said, trying to throw back a little salesman lingo. I then asked the usual questions about what was going and what was staying. "When are you planning on moving?"

"Well technically, I'm not moving. It's my wife who's moving, so not everything is going. It's a long story. Can I get you something to drink? Some wine, perhaps?"

"I'd better not. I've got a little drive ahead of me when I leave here."

"Where to next?"

"Home to Glendale."

"I work in Glendale at the Nissan dealership. When you're in the market for a car, I can get you a special deal." There was that big smile again.

"I'm pretty set for now. Thanks, anyway."

Just then a woman came into the room from the hallway and asked, "When are we going to finish, Santi? I've got to pick up the children."

The woman was dressed—or, I should say, partially dressed—in an overflowing black bra and tight black leather pants with knee-high black patent leather boots. Her hair was jet black, and fell almost to the floor.

"I told you not to come out while I'm doing business. Please go back." He turned back to me. "How long will this take?"

The woman just stood there defiantly, not moving, glaring at Mr. Gabrielli.

"It really depends on how much I have to count," I said.

"Look, can we do part today, and then you can come back—maybe tomorrow?" he asked.

"I've got appointments in another area tomorrow, but so far, Friday is free, if that works for you."

"Okay, Friday will be fine, but you'll have to meet with my wife. Friday is a busy day at the dealership. You know, starting the weekend early," he said.

"By the way, this is my wife, Gabriella" he said pointing to the lady in the high black boots.

"Hello," I said.

"Nice to meet you. I guess I'll see you on Friday. What time will you be here?" she asked.

"Eleven-thirty, if that's all right."

"Yes that's fine." She turned back to her husband. "Santi, please!"

As I went through the house, mainly the living room and dining room, I couldn't help but notice the opulence and garishness of the furniture that surrounded me. Mrs. Gabrielli was taking practically everything in those two rooms. I was left alone to finish in there while Mr. Gabrielli hurried inside to meet with his wife. It took me a while to complete my inventory, and by the time I had, Gabrielli reappeared wearing a conservative suit and tie. As he made his exit through the side door that led to the garage, he yelled back to me. "Thank you, Ron! Got to run."

"I'll see your wife Friday at 11: 30, then," I said, and I was off.

Friday rolled around, and there I was again at the two oversized doors at 11:30 sharp. Mrs. Gabrielli answered this time, wearing a full-length white summer dress. Her hair was tied neatly atop of her head with a two large red chopsticks poking out in either direction. Her image today was the complete opposite from that of my first impression.

"Hi Ron, come in," she said, with a warm smile.

"Hello Mrs. Gabrielli," I said, trying to hide the surprised look on my face. I had been expecting a lady in black.

"Gabby," she said.

"What?"

"Just call me Gabby, short for Gabriella. Sometimes my friends call me Gabby-Gabby. You know, because my first and last names are almost the same. But you can just call me Gabby."

"So, Gabby-Gabby," I said with a chuckle. "I just had to say it once."

She smiled her approval, and looked up from the list. "So Ron, where did my husband leave off with the inventory?"

"We finished the living room and the dining room, and it seems it all goes with you," I said.

"I'm leaving him with all the paintings. He chose them. I think they're awful. What do you think?" she asked.

"My background is as a trained designer and artist, so I shouldn't say anything," I said.

"So you think they're ugly, too."

"Uh..."

We continued through the rest of the house, and came to the garage. With most inventories I do, people say to me, "Wait 'till you see the garage, it's full of junk." This garage was the exception. It was the cleanest and neatest space I'd ever seen. Every piece of gardening equipment was hung neatly above baskets of toys labeled "his" and "hers." Cabinets were also labeled according to their contents. It was like a showroom. Sitting on top of the perfectly clean floor was a classic 1957 Chevrolet. It was in pristine condition, and looked like it had just come out of a time machine. Everything about this beauty was perfect. I was drooling over it.

"It's just a car," Gabby said.

"Are you kidding? This was *the* car of the fifties, my era!" I said with passion.

"You and my husband will get along just fine. He spends more time with that car than the kids or me. You might have guessed we're separating. This is just one of the reasons. But, I have to tell you we have something between us that will never change. He's a very passionate man, and when he starts something he's very thorough. Something takes over, and he's like an animal....I'd better stop. I've already said too much."

"Yes, well...how many kids do you have, and how old are they?" I asked, changing the subject.

"Just two. Chelsea is seven, and Anthony is eleven," she said, looking down at the floor.

Always trying to relate to my potential customers, I said, "I divorced when my two kids were about the same age. The toughest thing I've ever had to do was walk out that door. Time *does* help, and keeping your children busy will help, also."

"Thanks. I'll take your advice. Now I guess you'll have to see the final room. We weren't sure we should show it to anyone, but you're a professional and, besides, you've probably seen everything, right?" she asked.

Apprehensive, I followed Gabby down the hallway leading to the mysterious room, and when we got there, she produced a key that was hanging from a chain around her neck. I wasn't sure what to expect, but remembering how Gabby was dressed when I first saw her, I was ready for something unusual.

Before she opened the door, Gabby said, "This is like an exercise room. I'm hoping your company disassembles exercise equipment, but I must tell you, this is not the usual kind. We had many of the pieces built to our exact specifications, so please don't be too shocked."

Well, I wasn't disappointed. As the door swung open, I peered into the room, but couldn't see a thing. The room was pitch black. Then Gabby switched on the lights. The walls, ceiling, and the floor were all painted black. On one wall there appeared to be a metal ladder that stretched from floor to ceiling, and several chains and ropes with various size hooks hung from what looked like a track that traversed from one side of the room to the other. A bench covered in black vinyl was on a short track mounted to the floor. In one corner, there were different sized chrome poles laid up against the wall. A small, narrow cabinet that looked not unlike a pool queue cabinet was on another wall. I didn't want to ask what was in the cabinet.

"I know this looks strange, but it's really quite tame compared to what we have seen at some of our friends' homes. We have been trying this in the hopes it would help save our marriage. And it did help for a while, but now it's just become an obsession for both of us. We don't want to give up this part of our lives. It's just that the love has disappeared, so we have to separate," Gabby said apologetically.

"The lock is for the kids, I presume. Do they ask about the room?" I asked.

"Yes. They've asked, but we tell them it's just a room where Mommy and Daddy have our special time. Until now, they've accepted our explanation. Anyway, we've never used the room when the kids are at home. It's worked out good so far, but my oldest is getting suspicious. So when I move out, we'll change it to a game room. That's one thing the kids are looking forward to when they come to stay with their father. But we're still not sure where in the new house we'll set up the equipment."

"I have to admit this is a first. But, I do understand that sometimes certain measures are used to try saving a marriage. As far as disassembling and re-assembling the equipment, if you could direct our staff as to what goes where, it would be helpful."

"I'm not sure about your crew even seeing this stuff. What will they think? Never mind, I know what they'll think. No, I think we'll move it ourselves," Gabby decided suddenly.

"You know, if you are uncomfortable with our staff knowing about your equipment, I suggest you just disassemble the equipment and move it out to the garage. Then it'll look pretty innocent. Just another bunch of exercise equipment. They'll never know."

"Yeah, I think that will work. We'll do that," Gabby said.

◆

Believe it or not, one of our crew knew exactly what the equipment was used for. Word spread among the loaders, leading to a bidding war to see who was going to unload the shipment at the new house and get a look at the woman who was moving it. The only person the crew wound up seeing, however, was the tyrannical salesman dressed all in black, barking orders about the special handling of his equipment. All that was missing was Gabby-Gabby, the lady in black.

COMMON BONDS
21

Of all the appointments I'd done through the years, my next one was to bring a satisfaction like none other. My connection with the native peoples of California goes back seven generations, when my Spanish ancestors married into a local Mission Indian tribe.

Doctor, engineer, and Indian chief. I was to meet someone who fit all of these descriptions. Several years before, Mr. Brandon volunteered medical assistance to a band of the Kumeyaay, a Native American group known as the Mission Indians. Soon after, he began venturing to several other tribes that were in desperate need of his help.

MR. BRANDON CAME TO THE DOOR as I was just about to knock, and greeted me with a broad smile.

"Hello, William Brandon? Ron Crosthwaite from the moving company.

"Yes, please come in," he said, giving me a hardy handshake as I walked through the door.

Mr. Brandon was a tall man, well over six feet, with a deep and commanding voice. With his silver hair pulled back in a ponytail, he looked like a throwback to the sixties. He was wearing dark blue denim pants and a long-sleeved white shirt. A leather strap encircled his forehead, matching the moccasins on his feet.

The first thing I noticed prominently displayed on Mr. Brandon's wall was a full Indian headdress. In fact, everywhere I looked was displayed a reminder of the variety of Native American cultures. There were photographs and artifacts in every direction. In the living room, an almost perfect circle of chairs was arranged neatly around what looked like a ceremonial drum.

"I have to ask, which tribe are you affiliated with?" I questioned.

"What gave it away?" Brandon asked, smiling. "I'm an honorary member of the San Pasqual Band of Diegueno Mission Indians of California."

"I am a seventh-generation Californian, and my ancestors are traced back to that very tribe, I think, or maybe the Campo band," I said, excitedly. "In fact, only yesterday, I attended a Kumeyaay burial ceremony."

"Oh, my. Well it looks like we have something in common."

"As a matter of fact, I've written a story about my Native American heritage. You might be interested in reading it. I would love to have your opinion."

"Sure, I'd like to read it. But you must know your story can't be validated since there are no written records. It was all handed down by storytellers such as yourself, I suppose. Was this a story handed down to you?" he asked.

"My father told me what he knew of our connection to the Mission Indians, and how we were related to them. But when I wrote the first chapter relating the link to my family tree, I had to use my imagination. I did my research online regarding the legends and myths of the Kumeyaay people. As you know, the Mission Indians are a part of that nation, starting with the story that was told to me by my father. He knew only some of the family history, but it was enough for me to elaborate on what might have happened."

We began to share our stories about the plight of the Native Americans, and from time to time Brandon would bring out one artifact or another relative to what we were talking about. It was fascinating.

"You have quite a collection! I notice some Kumeyaay baskets, and you also have that beautiful Plains Indian headdress."

"I'm a collector of just about anything Native American."

We continued to pour over his vast collection, as he told me stories related to each object. I interjected with tales about my own family's history and my more recent connections to the Mission Indians.

"It's so great to meet someone who's as passionate about their place in history as I am," I said.

"Yeah, I feel the same way."

"I noticed when your appointment was scheduled, it was from an architectural office. Are you an architect, as well?" I asked.

"No, I'm a structural engineer. I am on staff for a leading architect in the city," he said.

"Here we go again! My first occupation was as an interior designer, working for architects. I had a special bond with the structural engineer at the last firm I worked for. He held up the building and I, the interior designer, made it function. Neither of us got the credit for the success of the finished product."

"Isn't that the truth? The architect signs the documents and yes, gets all of the recognition, but it could also be to his detriment if something goes wrong. I'm fine with remaining in the background."

"I guess you're right. Looks like we could talk forever. Maybe we should get on with the reason I'm here. Can you tell me what all's going and what's to be left behind?"

"As you can imagine, all of the collectibles will be going, and the ceremonial furniture here in the living room is also going."

"I was wondering about this furniture and how it's arranged. Do you hold powwows here?"

"It started out that way, but a real powwow has to be held on a reservation. I use this setting to hold meetings with my Boy Scouts troop, which works pretty well, and helps the boys get into the spirit. It's all tied together with their ability to survive in the wild, and earn merit badges as they progress. I've used this approach for the past twelve years, and it's proven very successful in preparing them to grow into responsible young men."

"Wow, a troop leader as well. I'm impressed! Looks like moving to San Diego is going to leave a void in the community," I said.

"They'll be all right. My assistant is also very much into the same passion I have for the Natives Americans, so he'll keep up the tradition with the scouts. Anyway, some of the items I'll take myself. The headdress, for instance, is very fragile. I'm making a trip this weekend to my new place in San Diego, and I'll be taking most of the valuable items with me."

"Are you going to be working for an architect in San Diego?"

"Well it's a little complicated. I'm actually going back to practicing medicine. Before my career as an engineer, I worked as a surgeon in the ER at a large hospital here in the city, but I got burned out after twenty years. Down there, I'll be working at a clinic not far from the Campo Diegueno Reservation. It'll be more to their advantage to have me nearby, and a lot easier for me in terms of travel."

"My goodness. An engineer, doctor, and almost an Indian chief. I could write a book about you!"

"Sometimes a man has to go full circle until he knows where he belongs. I think you've got plenty to write about without including me in your stories."

"Well, I do think it would make for interesting reading."

"What about you? How did you come by this passion to write about your family history?"
"I grew up in San Diego, and I never knew my family history as a child. I would actually go adventuring at the San Diego Presidio back then, but didn't know the connection.

146

Now, of course, I'm trying to catch up with my heritage. When I found my father after forty years, he brought me back on track. He had been keeping records of the family tree, and when I walked into his small apartment for the first time and saw all the research he had done, I was hooked. I picked up where he left off, and began writing a historical novel based on our family's influence on California history."

"How was your family influential in California history?"

I told him about how my Spanish ancestor came by land from Mexico with Father Serra as corporal of the guard to establish the first mission, and how his firstborn son by his Mission Indian wife became the first mayor of the newly established Pueblo of San Diego. Relating this story, among others, carried us well into the afternoon.

Brandon wished me well on the completion of my novel, and said he wanted to be the first to read it. I continued with the inventory until all was accounted for, and then I moved on to my next appointment, but not until Brandon and I had exchanged contact information so we could help encourage one another to keep pursuing our common interest in the Native Americans.

◆

It was awe inspiring for me to meet a man who volunteered his medical knowledge to the Mission Indians from whom I've descended.

The connection came full circle when my half-brother became an active member of the Campo band of the Kumeyaay. He still attends many of their powwows. When one of his sons died, a Kumeyaay burial ceremony was held following the Christian ceremony at Forest Lawn. During the burial the shaman pointed her staff towards the sky, indicating a hawk circling overhead. It was explained to the congregation that the hawk takes the spirit of the dead to the Creator.

TANGO Y MATÉ
22

A light rain was falling on a cool November morning when I rang the doorbell at a home in Alhambra, a suburb of Los Angeles. The front door was at the bottom of stairs leading up to a second-story apartment. The lace curtains on the door were pulled aside by a figure peering out at me.

I HELD UP MY BUSINESS CARD to let my identity be known. The door opened, and I was greeted with a smile and a handshake.

"You can't be too careful these days. Hello. Rafael," he said, patting his chest. "Please come in."

"I'm here to see Margo Sanchez," I said.

"Yes, she is my wife. She's at the university right now. I can tell you what needs to be moved to New York. Please follow me upstairs."

When we reached the top of the stairs, I was transported to an exotic environment. There was no lack of color displayed on the walls or on the furnishings. It was obvious the décor had not been purchased from IKEA. An acoustical guitar was prominently displayed, and from one corner of the room, a huge potted palm came sprouting out filling nearly a quarter of the room.

Rafael spoke with a heavy Spanish accent and a refreshingly formal politeness. "Can I offer you something to drink? I've just made some Argentinean hot chocolate. We call it *Submarinos*. It's delicious. You will like it. It's hot milk, served with a bar of chocolate on the side. Dark chocolate. It has to be *dark* chocolate!"

"Yes, that would be nice, thank you." This was a welcomed warm treat on a very cold day.

As I waited for Rafael to return with my drink, a classical guitar played quietly in the background. On one of the walls of the living room was a collection of black-and-white photos showing an Old World village and a couple locked in a passionate tango embrace. Colorful paintings were displayed on the rest of the walls, which were painted a deep purple, except for one accent wall leading to the hallway that was painted in what I would describe as bright persimmon.

"Here you are, señor. Enjoy," Rafael said as he set a tray of the chocolate drink down on the small drum-like table in from of me.

I took my first sip, and I noticed Rafael waiting for a response.

"Delicious!" I exclaimed, truthfully. Rafael nodded with a satisfied smile. "I love the music. Is it Segovia?" I asked.
"You have a good ear. Yes it is Segovia, my hero," Rafael said, excitedly.

"I once saw him play in person at McCabe's Guitar shop in Santa Monica, and I sat right in front of him. I was as close to him as I am to you right now."

"How lucky you are. I have never had the good fortune to see him in concert. You must feel very privileged," Rafael said, who was listening intently as I related my good fortune of seeing the master of the Spanish guitar perform.

"I do. Never have I had such an experience since. I was mesmerized watching his fingers dance across the strings." Then I focused on the wall covered with photographs. "I was noticing the grouping of black-and-white photos. Are they of your country? And the couple dancing the tango. Is that you and your wife?" I asked.

"You can ask Margo about the dancing, and yes, I took the photos of our beloved city of Buenos Aires on our last visit there," he said.

"How long has it been since you've been back?"

"Not since Margo got her job teaching at USC. It's been too long, maybe eight years."

"Now you're off to the Big Apple. Why the move?"

"Margo has been offered a job at Columbia University to head up their architectural department."

"Wow, that's fantastic. I'm assuming she's an architect. I worked for many architects in my first career as an interior designer."

"I wish she were here. I'm sure you two would have plenty to talk about."

"What about you? How do you get through the day? I noticed the guitar. Are you a musician?"

"A little bit of this, a little bit of that. But my passion is professional activism and photography. I took those photos of Buenos Aires. Come, let me show you what I do. Are you finished with your *Submarinos?* It's good, no?"

"Hot chocolate will never be the same for me."

"Ah-ha. That's good, eh?"

"Si!"

Rafael laughed as he led me to his office, where he brought out several large black-and-white photos showing protests and immigration rallies in the streets of Los Angeles and other prominent cities. He showed me articles he had written about the plight of the Latin Americans in the United States. It was obvious he was passionate about his quest to bring justice for the Mexicans and South Americans struggling with the system here in America. He showed me a photo of which he was particularly proud, and offered me a copy, for which I thanked him.

When I finished the estimate and was ready to leave, Rafael asked, "Can you come back to meet Margo? I'm sure she would love to talk with you about your common interests. Besides, she'll have to tell you what she is bringing from her office at USC."

"Well, I guess I will need to come back. When will she be home?"

"Do you work on weekends?"

"What time this Saturday may I come by?"

"I'll have to check, but Saturday sounds fine. I'll give you a call."

The following Saturday, I met with Margo and Rafael. The rain had stopped and the sun was shining bright, as it frequently does in Southern California. Margo was a regal-looking woman, tall, sophisticated, and attractive. She, too, was very polite, and welcomed to me into their home with open arms. I almost felt as though I were a member of the family. Then I was introduced to another Argentina treat.

Maté is a traditional beverage in Argentina. Often used to break the ice in social situations, it is considered rude to refuse it. This is what was offered as I walked into their home. The drink had been prepared by steeping dry leaves and twigs of the maté plant in hot water, rather than boiling water. It was brought to me in a hollowed out gourd with a metal straw. Reminding me of a variety of green tea, I found it something of an acquired taste, but very refreshing.

"Can you stay for lunch?" they asked.

Although it was lunchtime, I hadn't planned on staying for lunch, but why not? I had nothing else planned. They served a combination meat platter and told me that Argentineans are big meat-eaters. While I had slowed way down on my consumption of red meat, I had to be diplomatic. The food was wonderful. Something about the way it was seasoned. I've never had meat taste like that before, nor have I since.

"Congratulations on your new position at Columbia," I said to Margo. "I was told to ask you about the photo of you two dancing the tango."

"Thank you, I understand we have a work career in common. Which architects have you worked with?" she asked.

I rattled off the many well-known architects I had worked for and with, and she was very impressed. We compared our respective projects that we had worked on over the years. It was great to talk shop once again with someone who understood.

"And about the dance photo, yes it's me and Rafael. We love to dance the tango. Do you dance"?

"Yes, but mostly swing. I'd love to try the tango one day, especially the Argentine Tango. It's so beautiful and passionate."

"Then you should start right away. If I had the time, I could teach you the basics at least, but I'm off to my new position soon. And, what happened? Why are you doing this for a living? Don't you miss design?"

"I simply became overqualified. Yes, in a way I do miss it, but now my creative juices are for writing. I still do a project for friends from time to time, mostly graphic design. You know, a business card or a brochure. Nothing too complicated."

We continued talking through the afternoon. Somehow, when Rafael joined in, we were able to integrate our conversation to include him. I had found new friends in Margo and Rafael. Their passions for participating in life's journey had me caught up in their quest to change the world.

Margo needed to be in New York by month's end, and the time was closing in. Having made friends with my customers, I watched closely over the progress of their move. Unfortunately for them, they were about to suffer a weakness of the moving industry. Their shipment was delayed. Margo had gone ahead of schedule to get settled into the new apartment and to start the new semester at Columbia. Rafael remained behind to oversee the process with the movers.

After Rafael arrived in New York, he waited for the shipment that hadn't arrived on schedule. Then he called me to find out why the delay. I checked and double-checked, and finally found out that the shipment hadn't even left California yet. I got all over my company, asking for an explanation. Apparently, there were circumstances that couldn't be explained. Things got pretty tense with Margo and Rafael, but there was nothing I could do. I felt awful. There they were in the Big Apple with no wardrobe and no furniture. Margo had to buy new clothes for work, which came at an unexpected expense, and they were eating out practically all their meals.

After pleading my case once again to my company, they came up with a decent compensation for the Sanchez's inconvenience.

◆

A week later, their shipment finally arrived. They were both very understanding, and said they didn't blame me, but I still felt responsible, and sent them a box of Ghirardelli chocolate. At least the gesture made *me* feel better as did their invitation to come and stay with them whenever I was in New York. I haven't made that trip yet, but when I do, seeing the Sanchez's will be high on my list.

Once again I had found myself exposed to a new culture along with warm hospitality and a new sensation for the taste buds. Connecting with someone in the world of architecture and talking about familiar passions from my past was very special for me.

COCOON
23

Some people are either forgotten or they choose to shut out the world and live their lives in another place and time. I've never reached that point in which the here and now has no meaning.

Unlike many of my appointments, this particular one turned out to be anything but ordinary, and with an added unforeseen surprise. I confirmed the appointment on the phone, and then made my way to a North Hollywood home. The house was typical of those built in the early sixties. Made of stucco, it had aluminum sliding windows throughout. The yard was so overgrown with tall grass and weeds that I had to step over a pile of throwaway newspapers on the porch just to get to the front door. Since the doorbell didn't seem to work, I knocked. When I got no answer, I began pounding on the door, thinking the resident was either in the back of the house, or maybe in the garden.

I WAITED AND LISTENED, and then after getting no response I started to walk away. That was when I heard a weak voice coming from the side of the house.

"Come here to the side entrance," said the voice.

I approached the side of the house, where a shaky hand sticking out from a sliding glass door gestured for me to come forward. As I moved closer, I could barely make out the image of a smiling woman standing behind the dirty sliding glass door, which we both struggled to slide open. It took both of us pulling on it, dragging and screeching along the grimy metal track, to finally create an opening just enough for me to squeeze through.

Stepping into the kitchen, I was greeted by the smell of cat urine so strong that nearly knocked me over. Holding my breath, I saw several cats scurrying around, trying to hide from the intruder. Curiously, there were two stoves and no visible refrigerator. It looked like this room wasn't being used for its original intention with open cat food cans and un-emptied litter boxes everywhere. The smiling woman in soiled gray sweats introduced herself as Ms. Colleen Damon.

"Hello, Ms. Damon?" I said.

"Yes, I'm Colleen Damon," she said, tilting her head back to one side, all the while keeping her eyes focused on me. As she spoke she was no longer the lady in soiled sweats that helped me struggle with the door, but a woman with a majestic elegance. It reminded me of a scene right out of *Sunset Boulevard*.

I gathered all my good manners to return Ms. Damon's greeting in what seemed to be a special moment for her. "Very nice to meet you, Ms. Colleen Damon. I'm here from the moving company to give you your estimate." I did not quite know why I was being so formal.

"Yes, welcome to my home. Please follow me," she said.
She seemed to float as she walked on her tiptoes, ushering me into the living room, where she began to explain why the

front door wasn't accessible. There was a single bed pushed up against the door where she said her friend slept. She introduced me to him, an older man also wearing spoiled sweats. "This is Stanley Morris, my dear friend. He guards my front door for me."

"Hello," I said, politely.

There was no response from Stanley. He looked over at me from the bed with his eyes, but without moving his head. Then, for some unknown reason, he got up and began to run a very loud vacuum cleaner. Since the noise kept me from being able to conduct my business, Ms. Damon shuffled me off to a hallway, where she pointed through a metal security screen door leading to a bedroom. She explained that the reason the screen door was kept closed was that the male cats needed to be separated from the females.

"Too many cats. All they want to do is jump the lady cats. Would you like a cat?" she asked.

"No, I have no room for a pet, and I'm really not a cat person. But thanks for the offer," I said with a smile, while breathing into my shirt to mask the room's pungent odor.

"You live alone, young man? Are you sure you wouldn't want a pet?" she asked again.

It was interesting to hear this woman in soiled sweats speak so eloquently. It simply didn't fit with the image.

"Yes, I do, but I don't have time for a pet. I'm hardly ever at home," I said.

"Oh, but cats don't care if you're home or not. They get along just fine on their own. I'm going to make you a present of my favorite, Tom. He'll be good company. Remind me when you leave, and I'll get him ready for you. You know, you remind me of someone. I can't picture him right now, but I'll remember. You'll see. His name was Ronnie, and that's your name isn't it?"

"Yes my family calls me Ronnie, but I go by Ron. Just Ron."

"Well Ronnie, I mean Ron, everything you see in this room I want moved."

All that was in the room were trunks and cats and stench. She said the trunks were filled with clothes, which I later learned were costumes. She pointed to another bedroom, and, again, all I could see were trunks and cats. I counted thirty-four trunks, in all. There were also several racks of hanging clothes, some of which looked like ball gowns.

Back to the living room, where I counted another thirty-one trunks and twenty-six more clothes racks...but no furniture. The room was dark, with heavy drapes pulled across the windows, and not a sliver of sunlight was allowed inside. The only light was from two Tiffany lamps perched on two upturned trunks at either end of the room. The lamp nearest me had a rather provocative-looking bronze base, a naked man and woman in a passionate embrace, surrounded by vines climbing upward along their bodies. The second base, from what I could see, was equally as provocative, and looked like two women in the same embrace. There was eeriness about the room. It was as though time had stood still, and the only purpose of the two lamps was to light the hanging gowns displayed on the racks.

The paint on the walls was peeling, and large chunks of it had fallen to the floor, where a complex floral-patterned wallpaper was uncovered. Only where the light from the two

Tiffany lamps shone upward could I see the vaulted ceiling with its painted cherubs looking down from a dark blue sky and puffy white clouds that time had faded into a dull gray.

At this point, Stanley had stopped vacuuming, and was nowhere to be found. Without the drone of the vacuum, there was complete silence. The drapes masked any ambient sound from the outside world. If it hadn't been for the horrible smell, I might have thought I was on a movie set waiting for the star to appear, listening for DeMille to yell, "*Action!*"

As we started towards the dining room through a darkened opening, I noticed a faded unframed black-and-white photo over the doorway that had been stuck there with a couple of thumbtacks on opposite corners, and was warping toward the middle from the two remaining corners.

The photo was of Ronald Reagan, sitting with a rather good-looking brunette. The woman in the photo looked vaguely familiar, but I couldn't place the actress's name.

"That's me, with Ronnie. Ah yes, there it is. You're Ronnie. I mean your name is Ronnie, and there I am with you, I mean him," Ms. Damon said.

I looked again at the faded photo and back at the lady in the soiled gray sweats. It was her. Was my name taking her back to the time of that photo? Was she transferring me back to that time?

"Come, I want to show you something," she said.

She led me over to an old beat-up dresser in the corner of the dining room, and opened the top drawer from which she pulled out a tattered photo album. Inside was an old photo of her taken when she was a beautiful young actress. She stared at her youthful image for a brief moment, and then looked up at me with a curious smile. "Well wada ya think? Pretty good looker, eh?"

This photo was indeed of a beautiful young woman I had probably seen in one of those old movies from the forties. When I looked back at Ms. Damon in that moment, it was like watching a butterfly return to the cocoon.

It all made sense now. The trunks full of costumes, the racks of ball gowns, the darkened living room with the mood of a stage set, and the need for furry creatures to fill the lonely days. I found out later that her gentleman friend, whose bed blocked the front door, had once been her agent. He had stayed with her these many years, and was probably secretly in love with her. As I left, I purposely didn't remind Ms. Damon of the gift she promised me.

◆

I never got the call to move Ms. Colleen Damon. However, a couple of weeks after I shared this story with a friend, she mentioned that she had read a small article in an obscure local newspaper of an old actress found dead in her North Hollywood home. An unidentified man was found with her, along with thirty or so cats. They had all died from asphyxiation as the result of a gas leak. The police found two stoves with all four knobs turned on high.

I had been with a former beauty of the silver screen. To see how she wound up, as a recluse living in the past, made me thankful that my daughter, who was thought to have acting talents, chose to move on with her life, which included homeschooling her children and being a devoted wife.

THE MAN FROM COLOMBIA
24

I've never been to South America, but if I ever go, it will be to Colombia. From the visit I had this day, I was very impressed with Señor Medina, who represented his country with class and hospitality extraordinaire.

As I pulled up to the long circular driveway in an unassuming neighborhood of Monrovia, the only thing elegant about the property was the fountain at the end of the drive. The Spanish-style home had arched doorways and deep-set windows. Whitewashed walls contrasted with dark wood trellises, topped with lush green grapevines.

I ENTERED THROUGH A SMALL ARCHWAY leading to the main entrance, and walked up to the large dark wooden door. As I was about to knock, I heard a voice off to my right.

"Hello señor, may I help you?"

"I'm here to do an estimate for the Medina family. Are you Mister Medina?" I asked.

"Oh no, I am Juan, the groundskeeper. Is he expecting you"?

"Yes, at 10 o'clock."

"Please follow me."

I was led into the foyer and was asked to be seated on what looked like a weather-beaten bench from an old church. There were two huge planters on the terracotta floor with palms stretching to the eighteen-foot ceiling. A winding staircase led to the second floor. The adjoining wall was adorned with family portraits.

Just then, a set of double doors opened to my left, and out came who I presumed to be the lady of the house.

"Hello. I am Olivia Medina. You are Ron here to do an estimate for our move?"

"Yes, pleasure to meet you. Your home is magnificent."

"Thank you. Please come with me. My husband is in the garden, and we will talk there. Do you mind the sun?"

"I don't mind, but if there is some shade, I would appreciate that."

We walked from what must have been a family room through another pair of double doors out to the garden. There seated under a large umbrella was Mr. Medina, surrounded by lush tropical plants and a variety of palms.

He stood up and greeted me with a slight bow. "What can we get you to drink? We have iced tea or Aguadiente. Or maybe you prefer a beer?"

"What is that second drink you mentioned? Aquaden....? Sorry, I'm not sure how you pronounced it."

"Aguadiente. It's one of our country's drinks. Very delicious; you should try it." He sounded insistent.

"Sure. I'll try it. Thank you."

Mr. Medina was a man of about 5'5" with snow-white hair and a large full mustache that was as wide as his head. His skin was very dark, which made his white hair stand out all the more. He wore what looked like peasant clothes: all white, except for the bright red sash around his rather large middle, and he looked at me with inquisitive eyes. "You have Spanish blood, don't you...from the northern part of Spain," he asked, profoundly.

"Yes. How did you know that?"

"Your mannerism and your coloring. I believe if you came from the southern part of Spain you would be darker, like me."

"Well, I'd like to explain. I'm actually from both the northern and the southern part of Spain. On my mother's side we are from Leon in the north, and on my fathers' side, Osuna in the south. In fact, my birth name is Osuna."

"I know both those cities, especially Osuna. I went to the university there, a beautiful city. But I see on your card you last name is not Osuna. Can you explain?"

"My mother married a second time. And the name on the card reflects that unfortunate marriage. I only found out my birth name much later when I had to produce my birth certificate to join the military."

My preference for shade was directly connected with my skin color. I have vidiligo, which causes loss of pigmentation. I showed Mr. Medina a photo from my wallet of my son, who has the same coloring I used to have, and I explained how unhappy I am with light skin.

"I would never have guessed that you were once dark like me. You know I bet this change has opened doors for you."

I knew what he meant. That is, by having lighter skin I might be more acceptable in certain circles. "I would hope not, although I've never thought about it."

"Let me tell you of a story you might relate to. I once had a favorite plant in my home; as a matter of fact it was the very first living thing I was obligated to care for. I would water it and feed it, and when the rains came I would take it outside to drink from the clouds. I had that plant for six years before I got married. Then, like many changes, there wasn't a place for the little plant in the new home I shared with my wife. It had to be moved to the patio. After many days, my little plant began to lose its coloring and turned pale. I still gave it the care I had always given it, but, now and then, I would neglect it."

"My wife asked why I kept that old plant around. She said it looked awful." Medina took a moment to look around the garden. "As you can see I have many plants, and I still have that original one, but I no longer have that wife."

"How did you know that exact thing happened to me? How could you know that? I, too, still have a plant I had before I met my wife, and I, too, no longer have that wife."

"I think we are alike in many ways, my friend, and, believe me, I didn't know you had a plant you've kept and a wife you didn't. I was relating more to your skin color and how, despite your loss of pigment, you still have life."

Mr. Medina seemed to be a philosopher, and had a poetic way of expressing himself. It was refreshing and familiar, and I liked it. We continued talking while our conversation got deeper and deeper. The difference between us was that Medina had made some good decisions and wound up with a successful business. I, on the other hand, had turned left when I should have turned right.

After a while, Mrs. Medina came out to join us, and asked if I'd like more to drink.

"Yes, thank you. It's delicious."

The sun wasn't helping my state, and I began to feel a little woozy. That's when I asked, "Does this have alcohol in it?

"I apologize. Didn't I mention that? I must have assumed. Sorry. Are you all right?"

"I'm okay, but I'd better switch to tea, thank you."

"So, Señor Medina, why are you leaving this beautiful home?"

"It is time. We've lived here in your wonderful country for many years, but I miss Colombia, and we must return before it's too late."

"Too late?"

"I'm not a young man, and if I stay much longer, I feel I'll regret not spending my final days in my home country. But you are a young man, and still have a lifetime to venture out into the world, so you must come to Colombia, and I'll show you my plantation."

"Plantation? What do you grow?" I asked cautiously, knowing some crops grown in Colombia could be called into question.

"Coffee, of course. What did you think, opium? No, but I must tell you that my grandfather made it possible for my father to possess the most fertile lands to grow the finest coffee beans in the world. After the government shut down a shady opium grower, the land was awarded to my grandfather because he was an outstanding citizen in the community. The business was, in turn, handed down to me from my father. So, while I still can, I'm going to run the family business, and then hand it to my son. Of course, I must be fit to continue our tradition."

"I'm sure I've had your coffee at some time in my life. I love my coffee. Black, of course. Do you know which brand distributes it?"

"Our beans are in high demand from coffee producers all over the world; too many to mention. But if you've tasted good coffee in a fine restaurant, it probably originated from my beans."

As we continued talking, I heard a splash that sounded like someone diving into a pool. Within minutes I looked up and saw the girl from Ipanema. Dripping from the water, glistening in the morning sun, and walking in what looked like slow motion, this vision of loveliness came over to where we were sitting, and leaned over to give Medina a kiss on the cheek. She was breathtaking, with long dark hair, big brown eyes, and a body of the gods.

"Allow me to introduce Concepcion, my daughter."

Trying to compose myself, I closed my mouth, which had fallen open all on its own. "Hello, nice to meet you."

"Who is this man you are entertaining Papa? I like him."

"Now run along, my precious. We're doing business. Mama, see to our daughter, and have her put on some clothes."

Medina sounded a little embarrassed by his daughter's appearance.

As Concepcion was whisked off by her mother, she yelled out to me. "I'll be back. Don't go away."

Medina explained. "I don't like her choice in bathing suits. She's only sixteen, and she shouldn't look like that. Sorry for the interruption. She is another reason we must move. She's getting too much attention here in the States."

"I think wherever she is she will demand attention. Your daughter is very beautiful. A curse, I know, firsthand. My daughter is also a beauty. It's all we can both do to hope we've given our daughters the good sense to balance what God gave them with the right decisions, and not to rely on their looks."

"Hear, hear," said Medina, raising his glass for a toast. "To the curse of fathers with beautiful daughters."

We chatted for at least another half-hour, with Mrs. Medina rejoining us until it was time for me to do what I was there for.

The Medina home was deceptively small compared to the way the house presented itself on first impression. It was large enough, though, to house three bedrooms, a library, formal dining room, family room, living room, and kitchen. One other room that was adjacent to the three-car garage was one not usually found in a typical American home: a coffee tasting room. The blended aroma of all the various coffee beans stored here was astounding. In this room, Señor Medina kept his finger on the pulse of his business to the far south.

◆

Weeks after Señor Medina moved back to Colombia, I received in the mail two unmarked one-pound bags of premium coffee beans. They made extraordinary coffee.

I gave my beautiful daughter away a couple of years after meeting with Mr. Medina, and was grateful she found her way out of the jungle of temptation. Whenever I have a good cup of coffee I think back to my visit with Señor Medina, with his gracious hospitality and his philosophical way of seeing the world.

MOCKING GIRL
25

In the summer of '52, I was living with my mother and her new husband, the evil stepfather, in a three-story apartment in downtown Los Angeles. I would often go adventuring through the city streets, doing a whole lot of nothing with my friend Eldon, who lived across the alley from me. We were all of twelve years old, and one of our destinations was MacArthur Park, then known as Westlake Park. Our intention was to go fishing in the lake, using some thread and a makeshift hook made from a straight pin. On our way to the park, we had to pass by a local strip-joint that couldn't be missed for the pounding music that blasted from inside its open door.

A dark red velvet draped across the opening would billow open and shut from the wind generated by the passing of traffic down 7th Street. We would purposely slow our walk to almost a standstill as we passed those red drapes, trying desperately to catch a glimpse of flesh from the exotic dancer undulating onstage. The doorman who guarded the entrance to this place of sin constantly shooed us away.

My next appointment took me back to those innocent days when "a glimpse of stocking was looked on as something shocking," to quote a Cole Porter lyric.

A VERY WELL ENDOWED WOMAN ANSWERED THE DOOR. I forced my eyes upward, and tried desperately to over compensate for my awkwardness. Terry Mann was a bubbly woman with a compelling personality.

"The moving man is here," she shouted. An echo repeated her words.

There was no one else in the one-room apartment, but every time she spoke, there was that echo again. Parrots. She had two huge macaws both competing for her attention. They seemed to enjoy mimicking her speech.

She smiled, fully aware I was uncomfortable with the birds and her obvious charms.

Trying to not sound awkward, I asked, "Are you a model?"

"Not a real model, but every once in while I pose for a biker magazine. Wanna see? That's me." She pointed to a large poster over the sofa.

Sure enough, there she was in all her glory. Wow!

"I'm just a regular girl who happens to have a few advantages. It doesn't pay the rent though, and that's why I have to move. Besides, the landlord doesn't like my birds."

The small studio apartment reminded me of that place Eldon and I used to walk past on our way to the park, with similar pounding music playing on a tape machine. The walls in the living room area were painted dark lavender and the sofa was draped with a tapestry woven with figures of semi-naked women in all kinds of exotic poses. Over the sofa, on either side of the poster, were two red velvet drapes pulled back to reveal Terry Mann's poster, as though she were performing on stage. The walls in the kitchen area were painted a bright blue. Even the refrigerator was painted the same shade of blue. In one corner of the living area was a mannequin in full Victorian dress, topped with a large feathered bonnet. In the other two remaining corners were large white cages housing the loud, mocking parrots.

"So how much is this going to cost? You gonna give me a deal?" she asked with a flirtatious smile.

"Well it all depends on how much stuff you have, and how far you're going."

"Not far. I would like to move in with my boyfriend, but he can't stand the birds, either. Do you like birds?"

"Sure, never met a bird I didn't like."

"You're cute. You got a honey?"

"No...I better get started before you get me into trouble," I said.

"I know lots of girls...but they're all screwed up...never mind. Okay, where do we start?" she asked.

As we went through her belongings, I noticed quite a lot of provocative clothing in her closet. Skimpy-looking dresses and what looked like see-through veils in every color of the rainbow. There was even some sort of police uniform with ruffles.
"Will they take good care of my clothes, I mean they won't dirty them, will they?" she asked.

"No. We provide wardrobe boxes free of charge that you pack yourself," I told her. "These look like costumes. Are they?"

"You might have guessed. I do a little exotic dancing on the side. You know that club down the street? That pink building with all the silhouettes of girls on the front?"

"I think I came from the other direction," I said.

"Oh well, that's where I dance every weekend. You should come and see me. I can get you in for half price, or maybe free."

"I'm uncomfortable in those settings. If you don't mind, I think I'll pass."

"Hey, I'm going to change. Make yourself comfortable while I get into some street clothes," she said.

While she stepped behind a small folding partition to make her quick change before going out in public, I took another peek at the poster. "So do you know where you want us to take your things?" I called out.

"I'm going down to the club right now, as a matter of fact, and I'm going to see if they'll let me move upstairs. They have a couple of rooms over the dance floor, and I'm sure they'll be cheap. You want to come along?" she shouted from behind the partition. "Oh, that's right. You might feel uncomfortable in those settings...." Like her parrots, she was mocking me with a snicker in her voice. Then she said, "Can you help me with this...?"

◆

175

The early experience of peaking through the red velvet curtains and meeting one of those exotic dancers in person was a kick. It became a reality check for me. Terry was like those women who danced on the stage behind the velvet curtain I had passed all those many years ago. Meeting her took me back to my early exposure to the dark underbelly of Los Angeles. Today I got to look into that hidden world, where real people lived otherwise normal lives.

A WAY TO GO
26

Typically, a family of four to eight people would only need one of our company's moving vans. Many families' belongings would fill only a third to half of a van. But there's always an exception, and, on this particular day, I was to witness something for which I was not prepared.

This home was located in the San Fernando Valley, a suburb north of Los Angeles. With three bedrooms, two baths, and the usual complement of other rooms, it was similar to the other houses in the neighborhood.

AFTER I RANG THE DOORBELL, the door swung open to reveal a man who, judging from the state of his hair, had just come out of a wind tunnel. On the other hand, his flannel shirt and blue dungarees suggested a farmer, just in from the fields. He appeared to be in his mid-forties, with a full beard and a pair of wire-rimmed glasses perched on the tip of his nose.

"You from the moving company?" he asked.
"Yes, Ron. I spoke with your wife when I called to verify our appointment. Robert Johnston?"

"Yes, that's me. Call me Bob. Come on in. Please excuse the mess, but as you can see there's not much room to get around."

I felt as though I were entering a warehouse crammed with antique furniture. A maze of chairs, tables, and accessories covered almost every square inch of the room through which I was led to what looked like the clearing in a forest. There lay still more furniture: a sofa, a straight-backed dining chair, and a coffee table. The room was dark, and the only light came from a floor lamp at one end of the sofa. Tall cupboards and sideboards surrounded me. Bookcases and grandfather clocks were lined against the walls, along with Murphy beds, and unusual looking pedestals of all sizes and shapes.

"I'll bet you're wondering about all the furniture," Mr. Johnston said.

"Did you recently close a furniture store?" I asked.

"I know it looks that way, but no, I just collect furniture."

"Looks like we might fill up a van with all your belongings," I mentioned.

"You haven't seen nothin' yet. Before you get started, you might want to look around to see just how many vans you might need. Go ahead and start your business. I'll be right back."

I started to count what I could see. Clearly, it was going to take a while to get through this inventory.

From behind one of the larger pieces of furniture, a woman and a young girl appeared. They, too, looked as though they could have stepped inside from milking the cows or feeding the chickens.

"Hello, I'm Brady, Bob's wife. We spoke on the phone. And this is our daughter."

The little girl ran up to me, and said, "Hi, my name is Amy. What's yours?"

"I'm Ron. How are you?"

Amy wore a red-and-white checkered apron over a blue dress with shoulder straps. She had blond hair with red ribbons tied neatly around two ponytails.

"Right out of *Alice in Wonderland*," I thought.

Brady wore a flower-printed dress, and on her feet were black rubber boots. Her hair was hidden under a blue scarf that tied behind her head. "You'll have to excuse our daughter," she said. "We don't get many visitors. We home school, you know, and she doesn't see much of the outside world."

"Today is my birthday. I'm nine years old," Amy said with a smile.

"Well, happy birthday, young lady. Are you going to do anything special for your big day?"

"We're having a party in the yard. You want to come?"

"Now, Amy, Ron has work to do," said her mother. "Go along, and I'll be right there."

"Okay, Mama."

Just then, I heard a commotion coming from the back yard. It sounded like chickens, and maybe goats, as well. I couldn't figure out exactly what I was hearing. I looked at Mrs. Johnston.

"Oh, that's just Amy's friends. They're all just happy to have her come back to the party."

"Oh, I see." I didn't really see. It sounded like a bunch of farm animals, not a bunch of kids.

"I'll leave you to your business. 'Bye for now." Brady said, and then she vanished through the towering maze of furniture.

I continued my count. In the living room, alone, were six sideboards, twelve large bookcases, and four armoires. As I moved into what looked like the dining room, I had to find a path through a sea of armchairs and sofas. In the dining room, finally, was furniture that fit the room...only the room contained more than one set of dining room furniture. One dining table was stacked upside down onto another, and chairs were stacked almost to the ceiling. I counted twenty-three dining chairs altogether. *Where were the other dining tables?* I wondered.

"How's it going?" asked Mr. Johnston from the kitchen.

"Can you direct me to the bedrooms?" I asked.

"You're going to go back where you came from, then look for a door behind the green bookcase. That's Amy's room. Right next to that is our room. I'll meet you there in a second."

I was able to find the two bedrooms, and much to my surprise, each room contained normal bedroom furniture in the normal quantity. The closets, however, were something else again. They were stuffed with clothes, both on hangers and on the floor. When Mr. Johnston caught up with me, I asked, "Are there any rooms other than the kitchen I should see?"

"Have you been to the guest room yet?" he asked.

I followed Mr. Johnston to the back of the house where the guest room was located. It was filled to capacity. I couldn't even get in the door. From what I could see, there were several headboards and footboards, with dressers of all sizes and end tables stacked to the ceiling, everything held up by mattresses precariously leaning against them. I had to assess the content with a "volume assumption," Since there was no way to take a count.

"Anything going from the garage or the backyard?" I asked. I knew I had just asked a silly question.

"Follow me," said Bob.

We made our way to the backyard, and there was Amy with her friends: four chickens, two goats, a cow, and a couple of dogs. As I had suspected, no children. I noticed an old horse grazing nearby, but it didn't appear to have been invited to the party. Every one of Amy's guests wore a party hat; even the chickens and they were all eating the remains of a birthday cake. Amy, who was sitting on the ground, looked up at me and said, "Hi, Mr. Ron. I'm sorry, there's no more cake. Want some of mine?"

"Hi, Amy. No, I'm okay. Thanks, anyway."

I followed Mr. Johnston to the garage where he was standing before the open door. Like the guest bedroom, the garage was inaccessible. I did my best to guess at the volume. Then we stepped out to a Quonset hut behind the garage. In addition to all the animal feed, which my company could not ship, there was yet more furniture. There were even some very old pieces I couldn't identify. Their finish, or, in some cases the paint, was almost gone. Johnston pointed out that some of the items were from the Midwest and had belonged to his great-grandmother.

When we left the storage hut, I thought I was finished.

"I assume you don't ship farm animals," Mr. Johnston said.

"No animals of any kind. Are all of these animals going with you?"

"These are Amy's friends. Of course, they're going."

I went along with what I heard, but it did seem a little sad that all of Amy's friends were barnyard animals. Amy seemed happy, but something was wrong with the picture. However, it was none of my business, so I said nothing.

"Can you take the swing set over there?" asked Mr. Johnston.

"Yes, sure. It would help if you broke it down. And make sure you put the hardware in a safe place. Things like that get lost all the time."

"How about that lumber and the fence material over there, can you take them? We've got to keep the horse and the cow corralled, somehow."

"Again, it would help if you bundled it up for us. We can even take that piece of farm equipment over there, if you like. What is it, anyway?"

"I don't rightly know. I just like it. Now that over there is an old tiller. It's in pretty good shape, but I'm sure I'll never put it to good use. I still like it. It's going. Did you catch my collection of tractor seats in the shed?"

"Is that what those were?"

"I want everything you see to go. So how many vans do you think it will take to get this stuff to Wyoming?"

Before I could answer. Amy asked, "Daddy, what about Stewart. Is he coming with us?"

"We have to wait for him to come back from the war, honey."

"Is Stewart your son?" I asked.

"Yeah, he's over there doing his duty. He's on his second tour. He and Amy are real close. She misses him dearly. We're hoping he'll join us after we move, so he and Amy can be together again."

"Daddy, will Stewart die in the war?"

"Well, baby, we just don't know that. We just have to pray he'll be safe and come home to us soon."

"If Stewart dies, I'll die, too, and then I can be with him in heaven."

That stopped me cold. I had to get back to my equipment, which consisted of a small hand-held computer, a printer, and a tape measure. Excusing myself, I went back inside to the living room, sat on the sofa, and started to calculate the number of vans we would need to take this huge load to Wyoming.

Amy came in and sat down next to me. She started asking questions about what I was doing. I said that I was making what was called an estimate to see how much it would cost to move her family.

"What is that?" Amy asked, pointing at my small computer.

"It's a kind of computer. See, I select a category, in this case your living room, and make a count of how many items are in the room, like sofas and chairs and stuff like that."

"Oh, I see. That's cool."

"And after I've added all the rooms in your home, I put my computer next to this little printer, and with an infra-red light like magic, the printer prints what's on the screen. See...here comes the paper now."

"Wow! That *is* magic. Can I do the next one?"

Amy was full of enthusiasm, asking question after question. She had a deep thirst for knowledge about the outside world from which, I found out later, she'd been sheltered from birth.

"Can you take me in the truck with you when you go?"

"We don't take people in the vans, only things. Besides, don't you want to travel with your mom and dad in the car?"
"I don't want to go in a car. I want to go in a truck. Don't you think it would be safer in a truck?"

"Amy, what's the matter?"

"I'm afraid of looking out of the window and seeing things I've never seen before. I want to be inside of a truck with no windows, so I'll feel safe."

I was sensing something much deeper here. I knew it was time for me to stop asking questions and not get involved. Amy was starting to tear up, and I could tell this was going to escalate if I didn't change the conversation, and soon.

"Why don't you go get your daddy for me now, please?"

"If you promise me one thing, I will go get my daddy. Promise you won't say anything to my mom or dad that I don't want to go in the car. Promise?"

"I promise."

Mrs. Johnston walked in just as Amy was making her way to the backyard to get her father.

"Has Amy been talking to you about not wanting to go in the car when we move? It's all right. We know she is afraid of leaving the house."

"Has she never left the house?"

"Amy is not a well little girl. That's why we're moving. We want a better environment for her. She suffers from a rare disease. They don't even have a name for it, plus she has epilepsy. Hanging around barnyard animals is great for her immune system, somehow."
"How are you planning on getting her to Wyoming? I know this is none of my business, so please forgive me for asking."

"No, it's all right. I don't mind sharing with you. She is so special to us, and we want to make her life as comfortable as we can. The doctors say she may not live past her twelfth birthday. To answer your question, we don't know how we can even get her into the car."

"May I make a suggestion?"

"Please do. Any help would be welcome."

"You could rent a panel van. You know, like a telephone van. You've seen them. Or if you have the means, buy one. They have no windows on the side, only windows at the back doors, and you could block them out. It will take a little effort on your part to outfit the van with seats and seat belts, but it's certainly doable."

"That's a great idea. Why didn't we think of that? Thank you, Ron. I'll speak to Bob about your idea. I'm sure he'll want to try it. Thank you again."

Amy came in with her dad, and they all listened while I explained how the moving would go.

It turned out that three fully loaded vans were needed to get all of their belongings to Wyoming. They arranged for some of Amy's farm-animal friends to be moved in a truck designed for hauling livestock. As I had suggested, the Johnstons bought a panel van and blocked out the windows. Amy had some of her friends join her in the van to comfort her—a chicken, a goat, and both of the dogs.

◆

Amy's brother was pardoned from active duty after an anonymous letter was sent to the local congressman, telling him about Amy's condition and her love for her brother. Stewart was sent stateside to Wyoming to finish his stay in the army. He remained with his sister until she died in his arms just after her twelfth birthday. All of her friends were there at her last birthday celebration—the chickens, the goats, the cow, the dogs, and her brother.

How precious life is. One spirit, one family, one memory I'll never forget.

THE HERO
27

November 22, 1963 President John F. Kennedy was assassinated. Being stationed on an army base at Fort Ord in Monterey, California, at this moment in history gave special meaning to this world tragedy. Over 40,000 men and women in uniform marched to the parade field to honor our fallen hero. As we marched, there wasn't a sound of cadence to be heard— only that of pant leg against pant leg as we all kept time, like one giant heartbeat. There wasn't a soldier there who wasn't in shock.

The light rain disguised the tears that fell that day. I remember standing at attention on that field for the longest time, feeling neither the cold nor the discomfort as we honored our fallen leader. I had a pass for that weekend, and drove to San Francisco. There wasn't a soul around. The city was in mourning, as was the rest of the world. So I returned to camp to join my friends around the TV set, where we watched that memorable piece of history unfold.

That was over forty years ago. I hadn't thought of the military and what it meant to me until the day I was to meet a true hero, face to face. This veteran of two wars was waiting for me at my next appointment.

I RANG THE DOORBELL, AND WAITED. From behind the screen door, the figure of a man appeared from the darkness of the alcove. He was wearing a black robe and had bright white hair that jumped out from the shadows. His eyes were a piercing, steely blue, and his face looked as though he had been in the sun too long.

"Are you from the moving company?" he asked.

"Yes, my name is--"

"Come in," he grunted, interrupting me.

"Robert Mason? I asked.

"Yea, that's me." He said a with short deliberate grunt.

As he pushed open the screen door, I stopped cold. Next to him there was a large black dog quietly glaring up at me.

"Don't worry. He won't bite. His name is Jake. Just don't stare at him, and don't make any sudden moves."

I was led into his kitchen where we sat across from each other with my new appendage at my side: the big black dog, who was not letting me out of his sight. The kitchen table and chairs were straight out of the fifties with a plastic turquoise laminate top and chrome legs. The chairs were covered in a shiny light blue vinyl and had the same chrome legs as the table. All the walls were white and the cabinets were a yellow, picking up the mustard color of the linoleum-covered floor. There was a strong smell of bacon in the air. I was sure breakfast had recently been prepared, since it was late morning. When we arrived at the kitchen, I noticed there wasn't any attempt to turn on a lamp. The only light was from the morning sun streaming through the kitchen windows. Robert Mason sat at the kitchen table, with his back to the windows. His face remained in the shadows. Right away, he began talking about being a victim of the system.

"Did you serve?" Mason asked.

"Yes. I was in the Army Reserve, and stayed Stateside the whole time."

"Uh," he grunted.

"I was at Fort Ord when we got the news about Kennedy's assassination. It was quite a memorable experience."

"I was in Nam at the time. There wasn't a man there who wasn't stunned," he said, shaking his head.

Then Mason began telling me about how he had been wounded several times and how unfair his treatment had been since he'd come home from the war in Korea. As he spoke, his voice became louder and angrier. His face turned a deeper shade of red as the expletives came spewing from his mouth. I glanced over at Jake, the dog, to see if he was sensing the tension building in the room. He didn't move a muscle, just stared at me like he was ready for his next meal. I quickly looked back at Mason with an uneasy smile, and tried to add to the conversation but to no avail.

"Same thing happened to me when I got back from Nam…I got shot eight times in the gut. I almost died, but then I was patched up and sent home. I recovered, and there I was back in the game," he said.

As he unreeled his memories, my attention wandered to one of the kitchen walls, which was covered with photos of children of all ages, boys and girls. Most of the photos were in black and white, and the few in color were faded and discolored with time. As soon as there was a break in his story, I asked, "Who are all these children?

His behavior abruptly changed as he began to explain his relationship with the images on the wall. It turned out he was a foster parent to nineteen children who had all since moved on. Despite all the posturing and angry outbursts, this man was actually a saint. I began to relax as he looked back at me with those steely eyes, which had softened as he spoke of his extended family. He named them one by one, sharing stories about them, and seeming to relive those times gone by. Another glance over at Jake found him lying down with eyes closed, his huge head resting on his oversized paws.

"Have any of your foster children joined the military?" I asked.

"See those two boys there on the right? Charles and Matthew both joined the Marines and are still serving. One of the girls is in the Navy as a Communications Officer. I hear from her once in a while when she's out to sea on maneuvers." Mason's eyes wandered over the photos searching for another story to tell me.

"Do any of them look in on you from time to time?" I said, quickly thinking that maybe I shouldn't have asked the question.

"They're all so busy with their lives, but I'll hear from the girls more often than the boys. Except for Bradley. It was very difficult for him to move on. It's been almost three years, but he calls me every day 'just to check up on ol' Jake,' he says. I've got a feeling he's looking after the ol' man in his own way. They're all planning a reunion in July soon after I move."

"Is your move taking you to one of the children?"

"I'm moving *because* of the children. Well, they're not really children any more. Most of them moved to Prescott, Arizona, where I'll be moving. That's where the reunion will take place. They all seem to want to stay together, so they tell me it's time for me to join them. I'm torn. I don't want to move, but they seem to want me nearby, so I'm going."

"How many of them are married with children?"

"Oh, geez. Let's see…I think maybe all but one or two have married. Only six have children, but you can say I'm a grandfather. Isn't that something?"

"Do you mind my asking, was there a Mrs. Mason?"

"You don't think I raised all nineteen of them on my own, do you? No. I don't mind you asking. I guess it's natural to wonder if I had help. Sally, Mrs. Mason, was there with me during most of the upbringing of the children, but she died just before we adopted Bradley. It could be why he's so attached to me. I pretty much raised him on my own. It was tough when she died, but the older kids took over and helped a great deal."

"I'm sorry you lost Sally. How did she die?"

"Brain tumor. One day she was here, and the next day she was gone. It happened so fast I couldn't even tell the children until they got back from summer camp. It was very tough on all of us, especially for the twelve-year-old twin girls. It was a time of their lives when they needed their mom the most. You know, learning how to be a lady. I did my best. But I started to drown my sorrows in drinking, and that didn't help the situation. Fortunately, Sally's sister, Carol, stepped in and saved us all from me. She lived with us for the next three years, helping out with all the chores I fell behind on."

As our conversation continued, I found myself admiring this man in the black robe, and considered him to be something of a hero—not only to his country, but also to the many foster children for whom he had provided a home. He had given so much, and now he was alone with his trusted dog and very little recognition for all he suffered in the battles he fought for his country. I believe he was also a very lonely man, and I was probably the only company he'd had for a long time.

◆

I later found out that Mason had graduated from the same high school I attended, albeit several years earlier. After he got settled in Prescott and following the reunion, he sent me a letter thanking me for a good move and for letting him bend my ear when I came to do the estimate. He also wrote that his trusted dog, ol' Jake, had finally passed away.

Those days gathered around the TV set watching JFK's funeral march came back to me after that meeting with a man who suffered through two wars and was left to carry the burden of pain. It made me all the more thankful I'd managed to avoid the trials of war. Sheer luck, I suppose. He also made me see the value of family. Even extended family, as in Mason's case, was a way of finding a kind of peace while living with the haunting memories of violence.

MANGIA MANGIA
28

I have fond memories from the early fifties of my mother and a teenage me attending special dinners with my mother's landlords. We lived in a tiny house we called the matchbox, behind the main house on Arroyo Seco Avenue in Los Angeles. The Magnos were an Old World Italian family. Nearly every Thursday night, they invited us to have a homemade spaghetti dinner with their family, which consisted of Sam and Grace, their two sons and their two children, and their one daughter and her boyfriend.

Thursday was spaghetti day, and since the Magnos thought spaghetti was all most Americans knew of Italian food, they figured we would enjoy eating something we knew about. As I grew to learn more about Italian cuisine, I wondered why we were never invited to dinner on lasagna day.

Grace Magno, the matriarch of the family, was a very sweet and generous hostess. When I came home from school, she would yell out of her kitchen window as I passed by, inviting me in for some treats. I remembers her husband Sam, spoke with a heavy Italian accent. He did a lot of smiling, and would shake my hand and gesture with his hands a lot. At our spaghetti dinners, tradition demanded they serve ginger ale to drink. I remember they had cases of ginger ale in their basement, and would bring up several green bottles to serve with our meal. The bottles had no manufacturer labels, which struck me as odd. To this day, I wonder where they got the stuff.

When the meal was over, everyone took a share of the salad from a giant wooden bowl. Then the salad bowl with its remaining contents was placed before Sam. There was always a generous amount left for the 'master of the house'. I have since carried on that tradition with my own family.

MY APPOINTMENT THIS DAY was on a Saturday, and it was not my favorite day to be working. But it was a good time to catch families at home, so I did my share, and catch them I did. When I pulled up to my last appointment of the day, I found I was in the middle of an Italian wedding reception. Two men came towards me, both with a drink in their hands, and gestured for me to come in. It was obvious they were expecting me. So, I gathered my equipment, and I followed them into the house.

They apologized for the mix-up in the date and said if I would like to reschedule, they would understand.

"I'll give it a try, if you don't mind. I'll just work around your guests."

The reception was being held in the backyard, so I pretty much had the house to myself. Mr. Cangelosi, the father of the bride, introduced me to everyone who came to the house. Like most Italian men from the Old Country, Mr. Cangelosi had a thick mustache and spoke with a heavy accent, always smiling. He seemed to be especially happy about this celebration, laughing loudly following everything he said.

"This is the man who will move us to our new home," he said, putting his arm around me and laughing. Then he turned to me, and said, "Have a glass of wine, my friend."

"No, thank you. I'd better keep working."

"Come on. It's my daughter's happy day...drink!"

I smiled, took the glass, and raised it in a toast to the new couple. "To the newlyweds."

"Ah, that's more like it. Now you go ahead and work, and let me know when you're ready, eh?" he laughed.

This was a large Italian family with many guests coming and going in and out of the house to the kitchen. The smell of the food cooking took me back to Grace Magno's kitchen and recalled many good memories. I saw Mrs. Cangelosi as another Grace, so when she invited me to eat with them in the backyard, it seemed natural to join in.

"Come, take a break, have some good food. Come, *mangia, mangia.*"

How could I refuse? I walked out into the backyard, and was introduced like a member of the family.

"Hey everybody, this is Ron, our moving man," Mr. Cangelosi announced. Then he turned to me and said, "Hey, Mr. Ron, call your wife and have her join us."

"I'm not married," I said.

"What? A nice-looking man like you? Come let me introduce you to my niece."

"Mr. Cangelosi, no. It's okay," I said.

"You got a girlfriend?"

"No."

"Well come on, then. This is Gina, eh?" he said, laughing.

Gina was an Italian beauty, but quite a bit younger than I, so I just smiled and talked politely for a while.

"You must forgive my uncle. He's a little drunk. I'm sorry if he embarrassed you," Gina said.

"No, no, it's fine. He's a very generous man. In fact, the whole family is so nice to welcome in a complete stranger."

"When my uncle and my father came to America they were warmly greeted by everyone, so they vowed that they would try to repay the generosity. They've been this way for as long as I can remember. It seems a little overly friendly."

"I think it's refreshing," I told her. "How long have you been here in America?"

"I was born here."

"Oh, I see. Where in Italy is your family from?"

"A small hillside village in Southern Italy called Capizzo."

"Sounds quaint."

"They say the people there are very poor, and that's why my father and his brother decided to come to America to make a better life."

"Do they ever return home?"

"They haven't been back for a long time now. Each time they went, though, they would bring with them another family member. Now, they're all here. Everyone at this party is from Capizzo, except those of us who were born here. You know, the younger ones."

"This is a true American story. How wonderful."

"Have you ever been to Italy, Mr. Ron?"

"No. I've been to Europe, but not to Italy. My daughter has been to Rome, though, and she said it was wonderful."

Just then, as I looked up, the sun was blocked for an instant.

"Oh, this is my cousin Angie," Gina said.

"Hello. Very nice to meet you, Angie," I said as I reached to shake her hand.

"He's so formal. Come here." With that, Angie gave me a big hug like I was a long-lost family member.

Angie was closer to me in age, but she was twice my size. Gina excused herself, and left me with my new friend.

"I'm going to get some more food. Can I get you anything?
"No thanks. I've had plenty; maybe later."

As I got up to make my exit, someone grabbed my hand and began showing me the family's traditional dance. There I was, completely immersed in this family celebration, and before I knew it, I was back in the arms of Angie, who was whirling me around like a rag doll. I danced, I laughed, I ate, I drank…late into the afternoon.

◆

As a result of the Cangelosi family's generosity, I eventually got two additional moves; one from Mr. Cangelosi's brother Gus, and one from my dance partner, Angie Cangelosi.

So many years have passed since those special dinners with Sam and Grace Magno. I had forgotten how those days carried over to influence my family traditions, and enrich my personal development.

When setting down to dinner with my family, the big salad bowl was left for me to finish. I started drinking ginger ale on a regular basis, and Thursdays became spaghetti day around my home.

Not until many years later did I appreciate how the Magno family had greatly affected my life in this small way.

◆◆◆

www.ingramcontent.com/pod-product-compliance
Lightning Source LLC
Chambersburg PA
CBHW020854090426
42736CB00008B/369